HISTOR ✓ W9-BZF-575

VIETNAM HELICOPTER HANDBOOK

VIETNAM HELICOPTER HANDBOOK

Barry Gregory

Patrick Stephens

First published in 1988

All pictures supplied by Military Archive and Research
Services

British Library Cataloguing in Publication Data

Gregory, Barry
Vietnam helicopter handbook.
1. Vietnamese Conflict, 1961-1975—
Aerial operations   2. Military helicopters—History
I. Title
959.704′348   DS558.8

ISBN 1-85260-024-1

Cover illustrations
Front 'Hueys' over Can Tho, Vietnam in 1967: a door gunner scans the
rice paddies for signs of enemy movement.
Back A UH-1D helicopter provides support to Infantry preparing to move
out behind the cover of an M-113 Armoured Personnel Carrier in 1969.

Patrick Stephens Limited is part of the
Thorsons Publishing Group,
Wellingborough, Northamptonshire, NN8 2RQ, England

Printed in Great Britain by Baker, Land and Unwin Printing,
Wellingborough, Northamptonshire.

1   3   5   7   9   10   8   6   4   2

CONTENTS

WELCOME TO VIETNAM

On 11 December 1961, the United States aircraft carrier USNS *Card* docked in Saigon harbour with 32 US Army H-21 helicopters and 400 men. The 57th Transportation Company (Light Helicopter) from Fort Lewis, Washington, and the 8th Transportation Company (Light Helicopter) from Fort Bragg, North Carolina, had arrived in South-east Asia. This event had a two-fold significance: it was the first major symbol of United States combat power in Vietnam, and it was the beginning of a new era of airmobility in the United States Army.

Just 12 days later, these helicopters were committed to the first airmobile combat action in Vietnam, Operation 'Chopper'. Approximately 1,000 Vietnamese paratroopers were airlifted into a suspected Viet Cong headquarters complex about ten miles west of Saigon, where they captured an elusive underground radio transmitter after meeting only slight resistance from a surprised enemy.

The events of December 1961 prefaced a decade of unparalleled growth of airmobility, but they also were a culmination of many decisions taken during the preceding decade which allowed the President of the United States to exercise this option in support of the Government of South Vietnam. Early in 1961, General Maxwell D. Taylor, a firm favourite of President John F. Kennedy, had gone to South-east Asia to make a situation report. During the General's visit, he had decided that the lack of adequate roads, lines of communication and means of mobility contributed heavily to the government's problems in fighting the Viet Cong guerrillas.

As a result of General Taylor's recommendations, the President approved a more active support programme for South Vietnam to assist in the fight against the VC, who were controlled by Ho Chi Minh and his Communist High Command in Hanoi. Generally, the American support included the establishment of a joint headquarters to direct the programme, an increase in the number of US advisers for the South Vietnamese armed forces and additional support through Army Aviation, communications units and Navy and Air Force units. Thus began a chain of events that led to the arrival of the helicopter units in Saigon in December 1961.

Following the 57th and 8th, the 93rd Transportation Company (Light Helicopter) arrived off the coast of Vietnam in January 1962. The first two helicopter units were based at Tan Son Nhut, Saigon's commercial airport, but this time the USNS *Card* was assigned to Danang in the northern I Corps Tactical Zone. Ten miles out in the South China Sea, the aircraft were flown off the carrier deck to Danang Air Base. This unique delivery of H-21

Crew members have stripped a Vertol H-21 Shawnee 'Flying Banana' helicopter that crashed into an embankment near Cau Mau in December 1962, while a second H-21 provides cover for disembarked South Vietnamese troops. These helicopters were amongst the first to arrive in Vietnam on 11 December 1961.

helicopters was accomplished without serious incident even though ceilings were down to 100 feet over the ocean.

The US aviation companies were at once engaged in a heavy combat flying programme, but difficulties were experienced because of a critical shortage of engines and a deterioration of rotor blades and aviation equipment. The first Marine helicopter squadron arrived in South Vietnam in April 1962 and was established at the old French base at Soc Trang in the Mekong Delta. In June and July of that year the Marines swapped bases with the 93rd Transportation Company at Danang because of the greater ability of the Marine H-34 helicopters in the mountainous region south of the Demilitarized Zone (DMZ) on the 17th parallel.

In order to provide better command and control of the Army's growing fleet, the 45th Transportation Battalion was deployed to South Vietnam in early 1962 from Fort Sill, Oklahoma, and assumed command of the three Army helicopter companies and a fixed-wing UH-1A Otter company, which had arrived in January from Fort Riley, Kansas. Two more helicopter companies, the 23rd and 81st, made their appearance and were placed under the command of the 45th Transportation Battalion.

In the first months of 1962, the first of a long line of 'Hueys' also arrived in South Vietnam as part of the 57th Medical Detachment (Helicopter Ambulance). The growing number of casualties amongst the Army of South Vietnam (ARVN) and their American advisers had called for the urgent despatch of the 57th from Fort

Top *Vietnamese Rangers board US Army H-21 helicopters about to take off in the hunt for Viet Cong guerrillas on the Plain of Reeds in the Mekong Delta in 1962.*

Above *The same flight of US Army H-21s, airborne.*

George Meade, Maryland, to provide the aerial ambulances for the 8th Field Hospital, which was equipped for dental, thoracic, orthopaedic and neurosurgical care. Arriving in April 1962, the 57th remained on duty in South Vietnam for the next eleven years.

When the 57th, which was commanded by Captain John Temperelli Jr, was alerted at Fort George Meade, the unit was taken by surprise. As the Department of the Army had not thought to appoint a cook for the mission, Temperelli obtained a six months supply of C-rations, and since they had no survival equipment, the men hastily made up their kits from local stores. The typical kit, stored in a parachute bag, contained a machete, canned water, C-rations, a lensatic compass, extra ammunition for their personal weapons, a signalling mirror and sundry items the men thought they might need in a crisis.

When they arrived in Vietnam in late April, the pilots had five 'Hueys', as their UH-1 helicopters were nicknamed. Along with the 8th Field Hospital, the 57th set itself up in the seaside town of Nha Trang, 200 miles (320 km) north-east of Saigon. It flew its first mission on 12 May when a Huey flew up the coast to Tuy Hoa, a distance of 40 miles (65 km) from Nha Trang and picked up a US Army captain suffering from an extremely high fever.

The 57th were shortly followed by the 23rd Special Warfare Aviation Detachment equipped with fixed-wing OV-1 Mohawks to provide reconnaissance and photographic coverage in support of the ARVN.

Much of this activity in Vietnam at the time was classified and what information did trickle through to the outside world did not arouse much interest in the 'man in the street'. However, even if the halls of military power in Washington were not engulfed in any real sense of drama in 1962, the commanders and their staffs were already at work considering the kind of war America might soon be fighting in a little-known country in South-east Asia.

One of the keys to success in the Second World War had been land mobility. The principal means of deploying an infantry soldier

An American aviator briefs a company of South Vietnamese soldiers before a heliborne mission in 1962. A 'Flying Banana' is seen in the background.

into battle had been in a wheeled or tracked vehicle or on foot, and although some airmobility had been achieved during the years 1939-45 with the development of parachute, glider and a few air-landing divisions, these operations had met with mixed success.

In its broadest sense, the airmobility concept envisages the use of aerial vehicles organic to the Army to assure the balance of troop movements, firepower, intelligence, support — and command and control. The terrain in Vietnam with its highlands, jungled lowlands and tortuous waterways and swamps of the Mekong Delta, along with the monsoon season, presented real problems to counter-insurgency operations, requiring the swift dispatch of troops to a battle zone or trouble spot. So, although in the early 1960s the helicopter was thought by many to be an expensive toy and vulnerable to an expert with a catapult, a rotor-winged aircraft was clearly more suited than the fixed-wing variety, by virtue of its lower speed and greater manoeuvrability, for all-round observation in fire support, intelligence and command and control roles and for landing and taking off with troops in restricted spaces.

While the first Army aviation units were deploying to Vietnam, settling 'in-country' and making their first tentative tests in combat, there were events in Washington which would have a profound influence on the future of airmobility. The Army was cautious, but Secretary of Defense Robert McNamara goaded the commanders into action and asked General Hamilton H. Howze, Commanding General of the Strategic Army Corps and of XVIII Airborne Corps at Fort Bragg, to report on the potential of airmobility and the helicopter in the US Army.

The final report of the Howze Board was submitted on 20 August 1962. The air assault division was the principal tactical innovation; as compared with about 100 aircraft in the standard division, it would have 459. Ground vehicles would be reduced from 3,452 to 1,100, which would also reduce the airlift requirement for strategic deployment. Artillery would consist of only 105 mm howitzers and Little John rockets (airtransportable in the Chinook helicopter). Augmenting this greatly reduced firepower, the division would employ 24 armed Mohawks, primarily a fixed-wing reconnaissance aircraft, and 36 Huey helicopters armed with 2.75 inch rockets.

The Howze Board also emphasized the need for a new breed of Army aviators. Some 8,900 aviators would be required in 1963, growing to 20,600 in 1968. The Board foresaw an increased need for Warrant Officer pilots and recommended an officer-to-warrant-officer ratio of one to one by the end of five years. It also recommended major changes in the officer career programme to

11

enhance their training, administration, and utilization.

The recommendations of the Howze Board and experimental work at the Army Aviation School, Transportation School, Signal School and Aberdeen Proving Ground made possible the order to form an air assault (test) division on 7 January 1963. The test division, which was activated at Fort Benning, Georgia, on 11 February was named the 11th Air Assault Division to revive the colours of the 11th Airborne Division, which had included the first parachute battalions to be raised in the United States in 1940 and which served in the Pacific Theatre from 1942 to 1945.

Brigadier General Harry W. O. Kinnard was selected to lead the 11th Air Division and he handpicked his key personnel and gave them the widest possible latitude in accomplishing their particular roles in the mission. Lieutenant Colonel John B. Stockton's 227th Assault Helicopter Battalion — the first in the Army — spent much of its time experimenting with the flying of Bell UH-1B Iroquois (Huey) helicopters over long distances through low cloud and maintaining tight formation flying at night. Meanwhile, the Boeing Vertol CH-47 Chinook Battalion under Lieutenant Colonel Benjamin S. Silver Jr devised new methods of moving artillery and key supplies.

The newly formed 10th Air Transport Brigade, under Colonel Delbert L. Bristol, with a combination of the fixed-wing Caribou, a STOL transport aircraft, and Chinooks devised the first workable air line of communications. Throughout the early formation and training period of the 11th Air Assault test units, there was a

In this early shot of a Bell UH-1B Iroquois in Vietnam, petrol is being pumped aboard from a 55-gallon drum. The location is Tay Ninh airstrip, 50 miles north-west of Saigon. The Hueys were used as armed escorts for H-21s (seen overhead) while on combat support missions.

The H-23 Hiller was primarily a trainer but, as the CH-23 Raven, also flew reconnaissance and medical evacuation missions in Vietnam, such as here in 1963.

continuous cross-feed of people, information, equipment and ideas between what was going on in Vietnam and what was going on at Fort Benning. In addition, the 11th Air Assault Division formed a total of six airmobile companies that were sent to Vietnam during the testing period.

In March 1965, when President Lyndon B. Johnson had already committed combat troops to the Vietnam War, a tentative decision was made to convert the 11th Air Assault Division (Test) to a fully-fledged fighting division, and it was decided that it would carry the colours of the 1st Cavalry Division which was then deployed in Korea. Thus the 'Air Cav' was born, and in the words of General 'Jumping Jim' Gavin — 'I don't mean horses'.

Hundreds of pilots arrived at Benning in the middle of June, but until the end of July were told that there was no truth in the rumours that they were going to Vietnam. Like most Americans at the time, the pilots knew little or nothing about the political situation in Vietnam but they were eager to fly. During their nine-month period of flight training discipline was harsh and the fall-out rate high, but those with the right aptitudes relished the new and thrilling experience of flying helicopters.

Training commenced at the US Army Primary Helicopter School at Fort Wolters, Texas, where the pilot candidates underwent one month of pre-flight training and four months of primary flight training. This was followed by four months of advanced training at Fort Rucker, Alabama. The pilots did their primary training on the H-23 Hiller, or CH-23 Raven as it was properly known, primarily a

Above *A US Air Force Sikorsky H-19 Chickasaw helicopter at Bien Hoa Air Base in the Republic of Vietnam, 1962.*

Below *An H-19 medium-transport helicopter of the US Air Force lands a National Guard squad on a training exercise in the USA.*

The CH-23 was also in action in the thick of the fighting of the Vietnam War. Here a Raven comes in for a landing among tanks and armoured personnel carriers of the 11th Armored Cavalry Regiment near Bien Hoa in 1966.

trainer, but which also flew reconnaissance and medical evacuation missions in Vietnam.

A total of 85 hours of flight time was logged by each trainee at Wolters, then a further 88 hours were spent flying the H-19 Sikorsky, correctly designated the UH-19D Chickasaw, whose mission included transportation of cargo and up to ten passengers, together with rescue and observation operations (cargo was carried externally). During the last month at Rucker, each pilot would log 27 hours in the ship all were lusting to fly — the Bell UH-1B Iroquois — which in its wide-ranging roles was to be the universally recognized silhouette in the Vietnam skies.

When the pilot graduates reached the 1st Cavalry Division *en route* for Vietnam, they went through a rush course in combat techniques devised by the 'old salts' who had taken part in two big wargames in the Carolinas during the previous two years. Their speciality was low-level flying following the map contours, and to increase their confidence the pilots were taught barnstorming tricks like flying under power lines and making low-level turns so steep that the rotor tips nearly touched the ground.

With the Hueys, the most important technique for refinement was close formation flying. At Rucker, the pilots defined 'close' as

Boeing-Vertol CH-47 Chinooks of the 1st Cavalry Division (Airmobile) are seen aboard the US aircraft carrier USS Boxer *at Qui Nhon in September 1965.*

being in sight of one another, but now proximity must be measured in rotor diameters. In Vietnam, a flight of four Huey 'slicks' (the term coined for a transport helicopter) would have to fly, land and take off very close together from a small landing zone (LZ). Closeness meant from one to three rotor diameters, although in practice they flew at one or less.

On 28 July 1965, nearly 20,000 men of the 1st Cavalry Division knew for certain that they were on their way to Vietnam. On that day, President Johnson announced on television 'We will stand in Vietnam' and 'I have today ordered to Vietnam the Air Mobile Division'. The games were over. Life was getting very serious for the 'Air Cav'.

The division staged out of Mobile, Alabama, and Jacksonville, Florida, on the USS *Boxer*, three Military Sea Transportation Ships, six troop carriers and seven cargo ships. Approximately 80,000 man hours were required to process the cargoes of Hueys, Chinooks, Mohawks and Caribous crammed aboard the four aircraft carriers for protection against the sea conditions. The USS

Boxer proceeded via the Suez Canal while the other vessels crossed the Pacific.

An advance party of 1,000 men was airlifted and landed in the Republic of Vietnam on 25 August. They proceeded to An Khe, which was situated about halfway between the coastal town of Qui Nhon and Pleiku on the 100-mile (160-km) east-west stretch of road called Route 19, and which was to be the 'Air Cav's' highlands base in the heart of Viet Cong territory. An Khe itself was a tiny village two miles off the main highway, and here the advance party commenced work clearing the surrounding countryside for what was to be the world's largest helipad.

The ships dropped anchor in Lang Mai Bay, south of Qui Nhon, checked, loaded and off the ships on arrival. The vinyl coating during the second week of September after about a month at sea. Three days were allowed to get the helicopters assembled, applied to those lashed to the flight-decks was peeled off and thrown overboard, and boxes of rotor blades were brought up to the decks to be sorted out and attached to their mountings. More helicopters were stored in the hangars and they also needed assembling before the flight to An Khe.

While the choppers were being readied for flight, the pilots observed the Marine helicopter carrier *Iwo Jima*, which was also lying in the bay, with great interest. Marine pilots launched their huge UH-34D Seahorses, which specialized in supply delivery and rescue missions, off the rolling decks of their carrier, flew to the shore and then returned. For the 'Air Cav' crews it would be different: they would live in tents and be in the thick of the fight daily. The helicopters took off for An Khe with a brief stop for fuel at Qui Nhon. The US Cavalry was about to add a new chapter to its proud history.

ASIAN PRELUDE

The military helicopter was not invented as an expedient for the Vietnam War. Leonardo da Vinci had something to say on the subject of helicopters when he sketched an aerial-screw machine in 1483. The rotating-wing concept of flight has been pursued for hundreds of years in man's attempts to fly, and for much of that time it was considered a more likely contender for successful flight than the fixed-wing concept. Many ingenious small-scale models of helicopters were designed, but it was not until the Wright Brothers had flown their aeroplane in 1903 that primitive helicopters able to lift a man were built.

Between that time and the emergence of Igor Sikorsky's R-4B production helicopter in 1942, many experimental helicopters were flown in Europe and the United States with various degrees of success. One factor that contributed greatly to the development of helicopters was the invention of the autogiro by the Spanish designer Juan de la Cierva in 1923. Cierva replaced the fixed wing of a propeller-driven craft by a four-bladed rotor that was free to rotate about a vertical axis. The rotor was not powered, but was turned as a windmill by the airflow generated by the motion of the aircraft.

Development of the autogiro was suspended prior to the Second World War in favour of the more versatile helicopter with its powered rotor. The autogiro nevertheless paved the way for the German Focke-Achgellis Fw61, first flown successfully in 1936, and for Sikorsky's first successful prototype which flew in the United States in 1940. (Sikorsky, a designer of large aeroplanes and flying boats, had designed and built a helicopter in Russia in 1909; it lifted its own weight from the ground but had no reserve left for pilot or passengers.)

Once the basic principles of helicopter design had been established, development was rapid on both sides of the Atlantic. Some use of these aircraft was made in the Second World War, but it was in the Korean War (1950-53) that their value as military vehicles became fully recognized. By this time, the USA in particular was fielding numerous types of helicopters mainly from Bell and Sikorsky. Choppers were used in the Korean War for liaison, cable-laying, transport and a wide variety of other purposes, but their most dramatic role was that of aerial ambulance, evacuating wounded United Nations troops from the front lines to mobile hospitals several miles in the rear.

The first Sikorsky H-5 Air Force helicopters arrived at Taegu on 22 July 1950. Light fixed-wing aircraft had been having trouble finding suitable landing zones to pick up the wounded, but the H-5 had no such trouble in negotiating the mountains and water-filled

Above *An H-5 Medevac helicopter lifts out a wounded GI during the Korean War.*

Below *Wounded men are moved from an H-5 helicopter of the 3rd US Air Force Rescue Squadron in Korea.*

rice paddies and was instantly employed evacuating wounded soldiers from the battlefront. More H-5s were sent to Korea in a hurry and, as the war progressed, their effectiveness was constantly demonstrated in the medical evacuation role. The rough Korean roads made the evacuation of the wounded by land vehicle slow, arduous and painful, while helicopters could do the job smoothly and quickly, lifting the wounded to the Mobile Army Surgical Hospitals (MASH) sometimes in a matter of minutes. The helicopter was also useful in rescuing troops trapped behind the enemy lines; on 24 and 25 March 1951, for instance, H-5s worked with the then-designated Sikorsky YH-19 helicopters evacuating 148 paratroopers from the Munsan-Ni drop zone north of Seoul.

The H-5 helicopter had several operational limitations. It had no armour, its range was limited, and it carried only four people including pilot and co-pilot. Fortunately, the Sikorsky engineers produced the more advanced H-19 which first flew in November 1949. It had increased range, better altitude and speed capabilities and carried ten passengers besides the pilot, co-pilot and medical attendant. The combat performance was favourable and in February 1952 H-19s began replacing H-5s in the rescue inventory.

The H-5 had one further limitation; the handles of the standard Army stretcher had to be cut off to fit into it. Late in 1950, the US Army deployed four of its own helicopter detachments to Korea. These units, each authorized four H-13 Sioux helicopters, possessed no medical personnel but the crew members drew their rations and quarters from the MASH. At the height of the Korean conflict, Sioux helicopters succeeded in evacuating about 17,700 casualties to the mobile surgical hospitals.

A Bell H-13 Sioux light helicopter of the US Army being used for medical evacuation in Korea.

A Sioux in the process of evacuating a casualty of the US 8th Cavalry at Uijongbu, Korea, 1951.

The Sioux was powered by a Franklin engine and sported a large flexiglass bubble over the top and front of the cockpit. It could transport a pilot and one passenger, with two casualties on external litters. Although Bell Aircraft sent some of its test pilots to Korea to help the Army pilots obtain maximum performance from the H-13, it had not been designed for medical evacuations in mountainous terrain; its standard fuel capacity could not keep it aloft for the two or more hours that many evacuation flights took. The pilots had either to fuel at the pick-up site or carry extra fuel in five-gallon cans which could be carried in the cockpit or, more safely, strapped to the stretcher pods and left at the pick-up site. Also, since the battery in the H-13 was not powerful enough to guarantee restarting the aircraft without a boost, the pilots often practised 'hot refuelling' in the field. Although dangerous, the practice seemed safer than being unable to restart the aircraft near the front line.

Because the H-13D — to give the helicopter its correct marque — had no instrument or cockpit lights and no gyroscopic altitude indicators, most evacuation missions took place in daylight. Extreme emergencies, however, sometimes prompted the pilots to undertake a night mission by flying with a flashlight held between their legs to illuminate the flight instruments. The expedient barely worked, because the bouncing, flickering beam of the flashlight often produced a blinding glare.

When the first Army aeromedical unit in Korea, the 2nd Helicopter Detachment, arrived at the end of 1950 and put its equipment in working order, it still could not declare itself

Above *Sioux helicopters of the 45th Transportation Company await shipment to the USA at the Port of Saigon in September 1962. In the background are H-21 'Flying Bananas' which have been unloaded from the USNS* Crotan.

Below *This photo-montage of a Bell H-13D with troops shouldering a 'wounded' comrade below simulates an impending evacuation to a MASH base in 1954.*

operational because the H-13Ds lacked stretcher platforms, attaching points on the helicopters, and even stretchers themselves. The unit quickly received permission to fit platforms on the skid assemblies so that the stretchers could be mounted on either side of the fuselage and the Navy provided some of their metal, basket-like Stokes litters; covers were devised to protect the patients from the elements and secure them to the pod.

In July 1951, a new stretcher mount, manufactured by Bell Aircraft for the H-13, reached Korea. These greatly improved mounts accommodated a standard Army field stretcher, eliminating the need to transfer the casualty to a Stokes before placing him in the pod. Unfortunately, the covers that Bell manufactured for the new mount were usually torn up by the slipstream after just thirty days' use, so replacement covers were improvised from tent canvas.

Even with the improved pods, the external mounting and the absence of a medical attendant on the aircraft produced another difficulty. Pilots began to notice that many of the casualties needed transfusions before being moved to a mobile surgical hospital. In cold weather, an in-flight transfusion with the fluids stored outside the aircraft risked deepening the patient's shock as the fluid temperatures dropped. Then an Army surgeon devised a method for *en route* transfusion of plasma or whole blood whereby a bottle of plasma or blood was attached to the inside wall of the cockpit within reach of the pilot.

Since the Eighth Army possessed only 32 H-13s by May 1951, use of the craft had to be closely monitored and restricted. The detachments offered their service to all the fighting units involved in the United Nations forces in Korea, although at first glance it seemed that the language barrier would make many of these missions extremely difficult. However, the lack of air-ground communications helped in this respect, for it precluded any attempt whatsoever at spoken communication and a sign language was developed that was acceptable to all.

Enemy ground resistance to air ambulances in Korea never became a severe problem as it did later in Vietnam. Few landing zones were subject to enemy small arms fire, but many were within range of enemy artillery and mortars. In another respect, however, Korea was worse than Vietnam. Although the USAF destroyed most of the North Korean aircraft early in the war, the entry of the Chinese Communists into the war in December 1950 brought fast and powerful enemy jet fighters to Korea. The helicopter pilots were generally successful, however, in outmanoeuvring the faster Yak fighters.

In fact, whilst the Korean War was going on, American helicopters were also being used in the same Vietnam theatre in

An OH-13 helicopter prepares to take off on an observation assignment prior to a 'search and destroy' mission conducted by the 101st Airborne Division, near Bon Cat, South Vietnam, in December 1965.

which they were later to gain prominence, for whilst the United Nations forces were engaged in Korea, the French were continuing their fight, begun in 1946 in the jungles and rice paddies of what was then French Indochina, against the Communist-led Viet Minh guerrillas. The French approach to this unconventional war was prosaically conventional, but they did help to promote the military use of the helicopter.

The first two Hiller 360 light helicopters arrived in Saigon in 1950 for use by the medical service of the French Air Force, Far East. By 1952, ten helicopters were engaged in medical evacuation missions necessitating the construction of a heliport at Tan Son Nhut Airport on the outskirts of Saigon. By the end of the war in 1954, 42 choppers, all of American manufacture, had been delivered to the French forces. These included Hiller 360s, carrying only one pilot and one passenger, Sikorsky H-5s and Sikorsky H-19s, which were introduced towards the end of the war.

The little Hillers lacked power except for operations in the Mekong Delta area in the south and in the flatlands around Hanoi in the north. The H-5s had greater capacity, but could not fly at the higher altitudes required for operations over the mountains and karst that covered most of Indochina. The H-19s, however, were capable of flying anywhere in the war zone, and replaced the H-5s to compile an impressive record. Of the helicopters that served the French, virtually all were hit by enemy small arms fire, but only two were shot down.

Realizing the vulnerability of slow-moving helicopters, the French took certain precautions. A minimum cruise altitude of

3,000 feet (914 m) was maintained to keep the helicopters well out of the range of most rifle and machine-gun fire. Whenever possible, French pilots flew along secure roadways to their destinations, and fighter aircraft, if available, escorted them over hostile territory. The primary function of the helicopters was medical evacuation of the wounded, but they were also used for picking up downed aircrew and ground force stragglers.

In the mid-1950s, the advancing helicopter development in the United States was seeking direction from the military, and its engineers were making design proposals to potential military customers who were not at all sure of their requirements. Many new approaches to vertical (or near vertical) flight were being tested as a replacement for, or an extension of, the helicopter, and for the first time the US Army committed major research and development funds to aeronautic programmes.

Studies in tactical doctrine for the combat employment of helicopters had commenced at Fort Benning in the early 1950s. An infantry company, equipped with H-19s and, later, H-34s, was put through its paces, and as a result of a few months of concentrated activity a new field manual, *FM 57-35, Army Transport Aviation-Combat Operations*, was published. The basic tactics and techniques described in this manual stood the test of time and would be vindicated in the tests made by the 11th Air Assault Division in Vietnam in the early 1960s.

The first formal requirement for an aerial weapon for Army helicopters was initiated in the early 1950s at Fort Benning. The

This Sikorsky H-34 light transport helicopter newly fitted with Decca Mk 8 radar and flight log lands at Croydon, near London, after a flight from West Germany in 1951.

The UH-34E Seahorse, a utility helicopter of the US Marine Corps, demonstrates its ability to deliver ammunition on a training exercise in the United States.

requirement specified a lightweight, simple and flexible turret gun to be provided for all Army transport helicopters. Tactical experiments had proven the obvious requirement for some type of suppressive gunfire to be delivered by transport helicopters during the critical approach phase of a combat assault, and although the light turret gun was never developed as conceived, the Army was soon looking at other ways of arming helicopters. By mid-1957, a 'Sky Cav' platoon had been formed at the Army Aviation School at Fort Rucker, Alabama. This experimental team, led by Colonel Jay D. Vanderpool, acquired two H-21s, one H-25 and one H-19, and

An H-37 beats up the water as it strains to lift a 'Flying Banana' from a paddy field in the Mekong Delta in 1964.

A Sikorsky H-37 Mohave helicopter of the US Army in flight.

armed them with a variety of machine-guns and rockets. One of the most important milestones during this period was the development of the XH-40 Bell Utility Helicopter, powered with a gas turbine. Although designed as an aerial ambulance, it was recognized even then that this machine might turn out to be the most useful aerial platform ever put into production.

The early Bell XH-40 was standardized as the HU-1 and was envisaged then to be the replacement for the L-20 utility fixed-wing aircraft and the H-19 utility helicopter. Further developments of the Bell machine were planned to assume the bulk of the missions then performed by the Sikorsky H-34 and the

A crashed helicopter (Mohave H-37) which went down while trying to lift out a damaged Huey lies immobile in a clearing north of Bien Hoa, South Vietnam, in September 1965.

Vertol H-21, while the Vertol HC-IB Chinook was on the drawing-boards to replace the piston-powered Sikorsky H-37.

The early development of the airmobile concept was not without controversy. The search and rescue role in Korea and Indochina had been the responsibility of the Air Force, but the USAF were to view with dismay the Army's growing control over the development of the armed helicopter as a tactical weapon in the 1950s. From 668 light fixed-wing aircraft and 57 light helicopters that comprised the Army inventory in mid-1950, it saw the Army acquire over 5,000 aircraft of fifteen different varieties by the end of the decade.

When the war in Korea ended, the United States Air Force had units based all around the world to counter the perceived threat from the Soviet Union and the People's Republic of China. The mission of the Strategic Air Command (SAC) dominated the Air Force of the 1950s, and the recovery of SAC crews downed behind enemy lines should a nuclear war occur was a priority. The 8th Emergency Rescue Squadron, the first squadron to use helicopters for aircrew recovery during the Second World War, was activated under the auspices of SAC and based at Camp Carson, Colorado.

A NEW ERA OF AIRMOBILITY

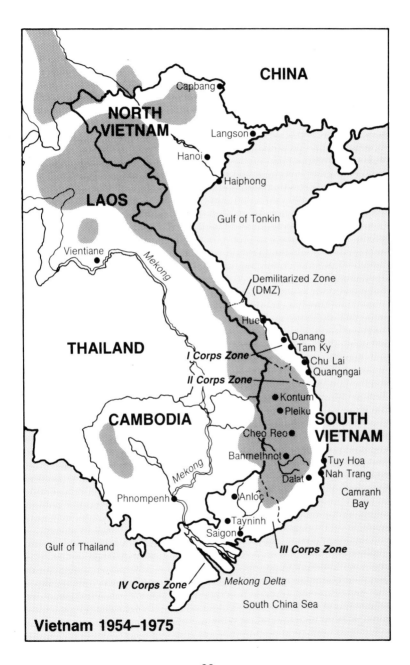

CHINA

Capbang

NORTH VIETNAM

Langson

Hanoi

Haiphong

LAOS

Gulf of Tonkin

Vientiane

Mekong

Demilitarized Zone (DMZ)

THAILAND

Hue

Danang
Tam Ky

I Corps Zone

Chu Lai
Quangngai

II Corps Zone

Kontum

Pleiku

CAMBODIA

Cheo Reo

SOUTH VIETNAM

Banmethnot

Mekong

Tuy Hoa
Nah Trang

Dalat

Phnompenh

Anloc

Camranh Bay

Taynnh

Saigon

Gulf of Thailand

III Corps Zone

IV Corps Zone

Mekong Delta

South China Sea

Vietnam 1954–1975

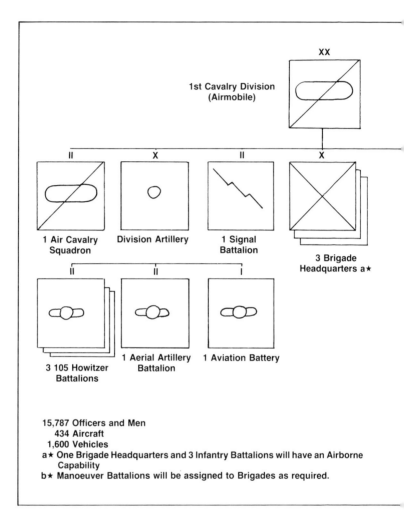

XX

1st Cavalry Division
(Airmobile)

II	X	II	X
1 Air Cavalry Squadron	Division Artillery	1 Signal Battalion	3 Brigade Headquarters a★

II	II	I
3 105 Howitzer Battalions	1 Aerial Artillery Battalion	1 Aviation Battery

15,787 Officers and Men
434 Aircraft
1,600 Vehicles
a★ One Brigade Headquarters and 3 Infantry Battalions will have an Airborne
Capability
b★ Manoeuver Battalions will be assigned to Brigades as required.

The Vietnam War cannot be divided into convenient phases. However, in the 'advisory years' from 1961 until 1965 the development of the helicopter at war went through certain definable stages. Firstly there was the learning period, a time when US Army pilots were teaching Army of the Republic of Vietnam commanders and soldiers how effectively to employ helicopter tactics, while at the same time the pilots themselves were learning by experience, trial and error. As more and more helicopters became available, more aviation units were formed to help the ARVN to become as mobile as possible.

The next stage saw the launching of battalion-size air assaults composed of selected South Vietnamese units, including the

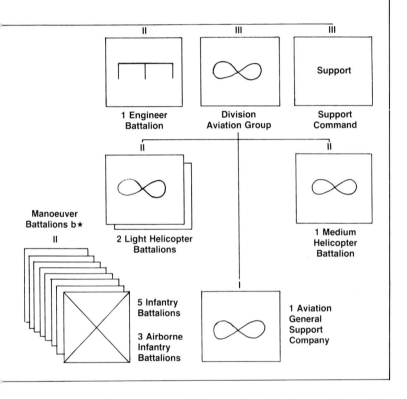

1ST US CAVALRY DIVISION (AIRMOBILE) ORGANIZATION

1 Engineer Battalion

Division Aviation Group

Support Command

Manoeuver Battalions b★

2 Light Helicopter Battalions

1 Medium Helicopter Battalion

5 Infantry Battalions

3 Airborne Infantry Battalions

1 Aviation General Support Company

paratroopers, the rangers and the regular infantry, and it was the success of this development that forced the enemy to increase their efforts in the south. The North Vietnamese Army was not unreluctant to take up the challenge, and the improved capabilities of the ARVN were matched step-by-step by the increased resistance of the VC and NVA, as additional units and supplies poured into South Vietnam via the Ho Chi Minh Trail and the sea route.

It was during this second stage that the US Army created its own airmobile division, tested it, and concluded that, in terms of ground tactics, airmobility was here to stay. The Howze Board had laid the foundations of the 1st Air Cavalry Divison (Airmobile) in the 11th

Air Assault Division (Test), and when the new division was activated on 1 July 1965 it was up to the 'Air Cav' to see through the job which had begun so well. Altogether, the Cavalry Division consisted of 15,787 officers and men.

It was also during this second stage that the Huey series came into its own. The turbine-engined helicopter, with its great power, its reliability and its minimum requirement for maintenance, was the technological turning point as far as airmobility was concerned. Actually, the key improvement of technology was the trio of the Huey, as a troop-lift bird, the Chinook, with its larger capacity for resupply and movement of artillery, and the fledgling attack helicopter — these together allowed the Americans to take a giant step forward.

The lie of the land and the guerrilla nature of Viet Cong warfare in South Vietnam dictated the creation of the new era of the helicopter. South Vietnam consists of three major geographic features. A coastal plain, varying in width from 9 to 15 miles (15 to 40 km), extends along most of the 870 miles (1,400 km) of the coast. This plain abuts on the second feature, the south-eastern edge of the Annamite mountain chain (known in South Vietnam as the Central Highlands) which runs from the northern border along the old Demilitarized Zone southwards to within 31 miles (80 km) of Saigon. The Central Highlands are mostly steep-sloped, sharp-crested mountains varying in height from 5,000 feet (1,500 m) to 8,000 feet (2,435 m), covered with tangled jungles and broken by many narrow passes. The southern third of the country consists almost entirely of an arable delta.

These three geographical features helped shape the four military zones of South Vietnam. The northern zone, or I Corps Zone, which ran from the Demilitarized Zone down to the Kontum and Binh Dinh provinces, consisted almost entirely of high mountains and dense jungles. At several points the Annamites cut the narrow coastal plain and extend to the South China Sea. II Corps Zone ran from I Corps Zone south to the southern foothills of the Central Highlands, about 62 miles (100 km) north of Saigon. It consisted of a long stretch of coastal plain, the highest portion of the Central Highlands, and the Kontum and Darlac Plateaux.

III Corps Zone ran from II Corps Zone south-west to a line 25 miles (40 km) below the capital, Saigon. This was an intermediate geographic region, containing the southern foothills of the Central Highlands, a few large, dry plains, some thick, triple-canopy jungle along the Cambodian border and the northern stretches of the delta formed by the Mekong River to the south.

Finally, IV Corps Zone consisted almost entirely of this delta, which has no forests except for dense mangrove swamps at the southernmost tip and forested areas north and south-east of

Saigon. Seldom more than 20 feet (6 m) above sea level, the delta is covered with rice fields separated by earthen dikes. During the rainy season the paddies are marshy, making helicopter landings especially difficult. Hamlets straddle the rivers and canals, and large villages (up to 10,000 people and usually surrounded by bamboo brakes and tropical trees) and cities lie at the junctions of the waterways. Altogether there are 3,000 miles of navigable waterways in the Mekong Delta.

South Vietnam lies below the Tropic of Cancer, between the 8th and 17th parallels, and the climate is generally hot and humid all year round. In winter the country lies under a high pressure system that causes a dry season in the south, but in the summer, however, rains fall heavily, varying from torrential downpours to steady mists (the monsoon in the I Corps area actually occurs later in the year). The northern region of South Vietnam has the highest rainfall averaging 128 inches (325 cm), while the Saigon region averages 80 inches (203 cm). In the northern region and the Central Highlands, where most of the fighting by US troops took place, dense fog and low clouds often grounded all aircraft. About ten times a year, usually between July and November, typhoons blow in from the South China Sea, soaking South Vietnam with heavy rains and lashing it with fierce winds.

Early attempts had been made to arm the Vertol CH-21 Shawnee helicopter, popularly known as the 'Flying Banana', which the US Air Rescue Service had acquired in 1956 as an Arctic rescue chopper (SH-21B). As a rescue helicopter, the SH-21B carried twelve stretcher patients and a medical attendant, while the CH-21 was armed with a light machine-gun at its door although the fire was relatively ineffective. The Shawnee nonetheless made its mark in the early years of the American involvement in Vietnam. In January 1962, South Vietnamese intelligence had heard of an enemy radio station operating near the village of Ap Bac in the Plain of Reeds. Fifty US advisers and 400 men of the ARVN 7th Infantry Division flew in ten CH-21 Shawnee helicopters to the area, five UH-1s that would serve as close air cover escorted the convoy.

The first three waves of helicopters dropped their troops into the landing zone without difficulty, but just as the fourth wave was touching down, Viet Cong opened fire with automatic weapons and shot down four of the CH-21s. A Huey moved into the face of the enemy fire to try to rescue one of the downed crews but it too crashed — the first UH-1B destroyed by the enemy in the Vietnam War. The other four UH-1s suppressed the VC fire, allowing the Shawnees to leave the hotly contested area without further loss.

Other than the unusually large number of forces involved, the battle was typical for this period: in the ground fight that followed,

CH-21 helicopters return to Soc Trang airfield after carrying South Vietnamese troops on strikes against the Viet Cong in February 1963.

the South Vietnamese infantry failed to surround the Viet Cong, who escaped under the cover of night. Three American advisers and 64 ARVN soldiers were killed, and unfortunately the 57th Medical Detachment, still stationed at Nha Trang and Qui Nhon far to the north, was out of range to evacuate the wounded. The radio station had been silenced, though, and there is no doubt that the VC realized for the first time that in the helicopter they were facing a potent weapon. Shortly afterwards the 57th moved to Tan Son Nhut Air Base in Saigon.

To meet the requirement for a suitable armed helicopter, the Army had formed the Utility Tactical Transport Helicopter Company and deployed it to Vietnam in mid-1962. This company was equipped with UH-1 helicopters armed with .30 calibre machine-guns and 2.75 rocket launchers and was designed to provide protective fire for the CH-21 transport helicopters.

Much of the tactical doctrine for armed helicopter employment was evolved during this period, including the techniques for protective fire and the preparation of landing zones prior to and during a helicopter assault. The Utility Tactical Transport Helicopter Company was redesignated the 68th Aviation Company and later the 197th Airmobile Company, and its early history was studied intensely by a special group known as the Army Concept Team in Vietnam which was established in Saigon on 6 November 1962.

The first element of 15 armed Hueys arrived in Vietnam in September 1962. During the period from 16 October 1962 to 15 March 1963, General Rowny, who headed the Army Concept

Team, subjected the Hueys to severe testing in actual combat conditions. Fundamental limitations were imposed, though, in the form of the 'rules of engagement' for US Army armed helicopters, which precluded testing of any tactical concepts involving 'offensive' employment. Under these rules, the armed helicopters could deliver fire only after they or the escorted transport helicopters had been fired upon. In late February 1963, the rules were modified to permit the armed helicopters to initiate fire against clearly identified insurgents who threatened their safety or the safety of the escorted transport helicopters.

Initially, the 15 UH-1A helicopters were armed with locally fabricated weapons systems consisting of two .30 calibre machine-guns and 16 2.75 inch rockets. In November 1962, the unit was augmented with 11 UH-1B helicopters, which were equipped with factory-installed weapons systems of four M-60 machine-guns per aircraft and locally fabricated clusters of eight 2.75 inch rockets. In this form the 'B' model eventually replaced most of the less powerful 'A's.

The provisional Utility Tactical Transport Helicopter Company was based at Tan Son Nhut and was under the direct operational control of Military Assistance Command, Vietnam. From this base, it supported the transport operations of the 57th, 33rd and 93rd Light Helicopter Companies, all equipped with CH-21 aircraft. In the latter part of the test period, one platoon of Hueys was sent to escort the Marine H-34 squadron operating in I Corps.

The first consideration of the armed helicopter was to preserve the safety of the troop transport. This 'escort' role was never precisely defined but broadly speaking it broke down into two phases. There was the 'en route' phase, which was generally flown at a safe altitude, and the 'approach phase', where the heliborne force descended to almost ground level several miles from the landing zone. The escorts preceded the transports into the LZ and remained until all the latter had departed. From the commencement of the run-in, the helicopters were at all times vulnerable to small arms fire, and when the LZ was small and the transport force used an extended formation, the period of exposure for armed escorts was unnecessarily long.

By mid-1963, the 1st Platoon of the Utility Tactical Transport Helicopter Company which worked with the H-34s in the I Corps sector had become adopted by their comrades-in-arms as an integral part of their operations, and few, if any, H-34 pilots elected to fly without the armed Hueys nearby. Procedures were developed whereby the Hueys picked up the fire support immediately the fixed-wing fighter aircraft broke off their support for safety reasons, and that, in most cases, was after last minute reconnaissance of the LZ by the armed choppers.

The Sikorsky UH-34D Seahorse was the Marine Corps version of the US Army H-34A Choctaw, and was also flown by the US Navy. It carried two crew and 18 passengers or eight stretchers and was unarmed. On 6 and 7 July 1964, the Viet Cong attacked the Green Beret Civilian Irregular Defense Group (CIDG) camp at Nam Dong in south-west Thua Thien province. Located at the junction of the borders of South and North Vietnam and Laos, the defenders had no tactical air support available, and their only hope lay in the unarmed helicopters which would have to run the gauntlet to come to their aid. Eighteen Marine Corps Seahorses and ten Army Choctaws met the challenge, delivering 9,500 lbs (431 kg) of ammunition, medical supplies and other equipment. The VC were driven off after three ground assaults.

When the UH-1B transport helicopter was first introduced in Vietnam, it usually carried ten combat-equipped Vietnamese soldiers. When ten soldiers were loaded into the Huey with a full fuel load, a US Army crew of four, armour plate, a tool box, a container of water, a case of emergency rations, weapons and armoured vests for the crew, it was grossly over the maximum operational weight. Not only that, but the centre of gravity shifted beyond the safe limits. As a consequence, the standard procedure was to limit the UH-1B to eight combat troops except in grave emergencies. It was also directed that the armed helicopter would carry no more than the normal complement of five personnel and armament with the basic load.

The lack of heavy enemy air defence had much to do with the selection of flight altitudes. During the early years, flights were made at 1,500 feet (456 m) to reduce the chances of being hit by ground fire. Various companies used different helicopter formations *en route* to a combat assault, and a major consideration in the selection of a formation was the size and shape of the landing zone and the company commander's requirements for disembarking his troops after landing. A modified trail formation was sometimes used when an uninterrupted flow of troops into a small landing area was desired. The formation most frequently used was the 'V', which proved to be versatile and easy to control, and also permitted landing of the flight in a minimum of time without bunching.

Helicopters normally flew about 45 degrees to the side and rear of the lead ship and high enough to be out of the rotor wash, while armed helicopters operated at the same altitude as the escorted force. A reconnaissance element of two or four armed helicopters preceded the transports by one to five minutes while the remaining escorts normally flanked the transports in a trail formation. If additional armed ships were available, they were positioned in the rear of the transports to engage targets under the flight.

A UH-1B Huey brings in 50-gallon water-drums to an outpost on Black Virgin Mountain, a Viet Cong stronghold, just 60 miles north-west of Saigon.

The helicopter companies always attempted to plan return routes that were different from the approach routes. For subsequent lifts, routes were varied slightly to avoid flying over a given area more than once, and, if one landing zone was used several times, the final approach and entry for each lift was varied if at all possible. In mountainous areas and in some jungle areas, it was not possible to vary the route of approach; consequently, every attempt was made to land the troops in the shortest possible time to minimize danger.

The critical approach phase was initiated by all transport helicopters at the same time in an attempt to place all aircraft on the ground simultaneously. This was difficult to accomplish because of the stepped altitude of the formation, the rotor wash encountered during descent, and the difficulty in finding a suitable touchdown spot for each ship — however, it remained a goal. The terrain in the landing zone sometimes slowed the disembarking of troops — in the Mekong Delta, for example, water was often chest deep and the ship had to maintain a low hover with the skids just beneath the water level, while in jungle areas, grass taller than the average man was encountered. Two minutes from the moment the first helicopter touched down until the last ship lifted off was considered average unloading time for a 12-ship formation.

To lessen the possibility of fire being concentrated on a single ship, all helicopters attempted to depart at the same time. Direction of take-off was varied for subsequent flights, and whenever possible the armed escorts used the same tactics on both the approach and return routes with the exception that the ships originally used for reconnaissance were the last to leave the landing zone and consequently usually brought up the rear. If another lift was required, the formation returned to the loading area for troops and, if necessary, the aircraft were refuelled and rearmed.

By November 1964, all helicopter companies in South Vietnam had organized their own 'Eagle Flight' formations, air assault teams constantly on alert. Each infantry company had at least one such flight in an alert status; the Vietnamese troop commanders were particularly enthusiastic about the arrangement for it provided a very close working relationship between the air and ground elements, and a special *esprit de corps* was built up from the day-to-day operations. A typical 'Eagle Flight' would consist of the following: one armed Huey would serve as the command and control ship and would have the US Army aviation commander and the Republic of Vietnam troop commander aboard; seven unarmed Hueys were used to transport the combat elements; five armed Hueys gave the fire support and escort to the troop-carrying helicopters; and one Huey was usually designated as a medical evacuation ship.

The 'Eagle Flights' were usually kept on a standby basis or sometimes even airborne searching for their own targets. Not only were the 'Eagle Flights' immediately available for those missions which required a minimum of planning, but they also provided the basis for larger operations. Sometimes several were used against targets that, when developed, proved too large for a single unit.

Simply stated, the 'Eagle Flight' was a microcosm of the large airmobile assaults that were destined to take place later. It had all the attributes of a true airmobile force with the self-contained reconnaissance and surveillance ability, firepower, and infantry troops. Above all, these early 'Eagle Flights' were able to capitalize on the element of surprise which was so often lost in the detailed planning cycle with ARVN forces.

Three other helicopters were employed in the pre-1965 line-up of US aircraft in Vietnam. At the beginning of 1964, the United States had 248 helicopters 'in-country', which included nine US Army Sikorsky CH-37A Mohaves. This cargo, equipment and troop carrier was first placed in service in 1956, and could accommodate pilot, co-pilot, equipment operator and 23 passengers or 24 stretcher cases. Its payload was 5,300 lbs (2,404 kg) and it could carry an external cargo of 10,000 lbs (4,536 kg).

In the early 1960s, the Kaman HH-43 Huskie, a short range (220 mile/354 km) helicopter, was the only crash rescue helicopter in the US Air Force inventory. However, local base rescue units in the United States and overseas which operated the HH-43

Crew members load rockets into the launchers of a Bell UH-1B Iroquois in Vietnam, September 1964.

considered it inadequate for duty in South-east Asia and the loss of two American aircraft within 24 hours over northern Laos urged the Joint Chiefs of Staff to hasten the dispatch of Rescue Service units to Vietnam. As a result of a directive in May, two HH-43Bs together with their crews and mechanics were sent from the 33rd Air Rescue Squadron at Naha Air Station, Okinawa, to Bien Hoa. In the event, the Huskies were diverted and re-routed to Nakhon Phanom Royal Thai Air Force Base on the Thai-Laos border. At the same time, Marine H-34s at Khe Sanh were also alerted for Air Rescue Service.

The HH-43B was a turbine-powered development of the earlier HH-43 piston-engined series and the first production model flew in December 1958. One interesting feature of the Huskie was introduced in 1961 when a new type of rotor blade was fitted,

A Bell UH-1A Iroquois fires a couple of HEAT rockets at a target on a firing range 35 miles north-east of Korat, Thailand, in August 1963.

made entirely of glass fibre. Another feature of the HH-43B was that it had twice the cabin space and payload capacity of the HH-43A, the increased space having been made by mounting the lighter and more compact turbine engine above the cabin and between the rotor pylons, instead of at the rear of the cabin. The Huskie accommodated two crew and six passengers and was not armed.

On 1 October 1961, the Air Rescue Service in the USA integrated 70 local base units into its structure. These utilized 69 H-43Bs, 17 piston-driven H-43As, 58 H-19Bs and four SH-21Bs. A handful of Sikorsky H-19s (US Army name Chickasaw) from the US Air Rescue Service stateside arrived at Udorn in June 1962. The H-19, which had seen service in Korea, Indochina and featured in pilot training was the Sikorsky S-55; it was adopted by the USAF, US Army Field Forces, US Navy, US Marine Corps and US Coast Guard, and flew in British colours with the Royal Air Force and Royal Navy as the Westland Whirlwind.

BELL AH-1 HUEYCOBRA

(AH-1G, AH-1J)

Origin Bell Aerospace Corporation, Buffalo 5, New York; **Mission** *En route* escort reconnaissance, direct fire support; **Service** (AH-1G) US Army, (AH-1J) US Marine Corps.

AH-1G HUEY COBRA LYCOMING

Engine T53-L-13 1,400 shp (derated to 1,100 shp) shaft-turbine; **Rotor diameter** 44 ft (13.41 m); **Overall length** 52 ft 11½ in (16.14 m); **Skid track** 7 ft (2.13 m); **Overall height** 13 ft 5½ in (4.1 m); **Weight** (empty) 6,096 lbs (2,765 kg), (loaded) 9,500 lbs (4,309 kg); **Maximum speed** (loaded, at sea level) 219 mph (352 km/h); **Cruising speed** (loaded) 205 mph (330 km/h); **Range** (loaded, no reserves) 387 miles (622 km); **Armament** GAU 2B/A (formerly XM-134) minigun six-barrel 7.62 mm machine-gun with 8,000 rounds; TAT-102A turret superseded on AH-1G by XM-28 subsystem, mounting either two miniguns with 4,000 rounds each, two XM-129 (similar to XM-75 40 mm grenade launchers) with 300 rounds each or one minigun and one XM-129; four external stores attachments beneath stub-wings accommodating various loads including a total of 76 2.75 in rockets in four XM-159 packs, 28 similar rockets in four XM-157 packs, two XM-18E1 minigun pods, one XM-35 20 mm gun kit, or two pods each containing four TOW wire-guided missiles; **Accommodation** Crew of two (pilot and co-pilot/gunner), no passengers.

AH-1J SEACOBRA

Engine Twin engine, Pratt & Whitney (UACL) T400-CP-400 1,800 shp coupled free-turbine/shaft-turbine power plant; **Rotor diameter** 44 ft (13.41 m); **Overall length** 53 ft 4 in (16.25 m); **Skid track** 7 ft (2.13 m); **Overall height** 13 ft 8 in (4.16 m); **Weight** (empty) 6,518 lbs (2,956 kg), (loaded) 10,000 lbs (4,536 kg); **Maximum speed** (loaded, at sea level) 207 mph (333 km/h); **Cruising speed** (loaded) 202 mph (325 km/h); **Range** (loaded, no reserves) 359 miles (578 km); **Armament** Electrically-driven 20 mm turret system, developed by the General Electric Company, faired into the forward lower fuselage housing one XM-197 three-barrel weapon, a lightweight version of the General Electric M-61 cannon (M-61A1 20 mm Vulcan) (structured provision in the AH-1 airframe also given for a three-barrel 30 mm turret system); four external stores attachment points beneath stub-wings accommodating various loads, including XM-18E1 7.62 mm minigun pods as well as 2.75 in folding fin rockets in either 7-tube (XM-157) or 19-tube (XM-159) packs; **Accommodation** Crew of two (pilot and co-pilot/gunner), no passengers.

The HueyCobra came into being as the result of an urgent programme initiated by the US Army when the Vietnam War revealed the need for a fast, well-armed helicopter to provide escort and fire support for the CH-47A Chinook. None of the helicopters then existing in the Army inventory had the ideal

A Bell AH-1G 'Cobra' gunship from the 2nd Bn, 20th Aerial Rocket Artillery, 1st Cavalry Division (Airmobile), prepares to fire in suppport of Skytroopers near Phuoc Vinh in 1969.

qualities for the job. The first HueyCobra (AH-1G) arrived in Vietnam on 1 September 1967, and the initial six aircraft were assigned to New Equipment Training Teams under the supervision of the 1st Aviation Brigade. Cobra New Equipment Training Team training started on 18 September with pilot transition courses and instruction on airframe, engine, armament and avionics maintenance.

The Bell Model 209 (single-engined) HueyCobra, designated AH-1G by the US Army, first flew on 7 September 1965, six months after its development was started, and was a direct development of the UH-1B/1C Iroquois (see page 50) intended specifically for armed missions. It combined the basic transmission and rotor system and (in its standard form) the power plant of the UH-1C with a new streamlined fuselage designed for maximum speed, armament load and crew efficiency. The prototype was sent to Edwards Air Force Base for US Army evaluation in December 1965, then, on 11 March 1966, the Army announced its intention to order the HueyCobra into production.

By October 1968 the Army had 838 on order, most of which had been delivered by the autumn of the following year, then on 30 January 1970 the Army ordered a further 170 AH-1Gs for delivery between July 1971 and August 1972. Deliveries of the original production series began in June 1967 and operational deployment in Vietnam followed a few months later. The US Marine Corps acquired 38 AH-1Gs for transition training and initial deployment pending the delivery of the twin-engined AH-1J (described below).

Relatively small, the HueyCobra had a low silhouette and narrow profile, with a fuselage width of only 3 ft (91 cm). Although the noise of their rotors betrayed approaching helicopters, these features helped to conceal the 'Snakes' (to use the Cobra's Vietnam nickname) when approaching a landing zone and on the ground where they could be hastily covered by the camouflage nets or moved into the cover of trees. The greater agility of the armed helicopter, as compared with the fixed-wing aircraft, and the AH-1G's performance in speed and manoeuvrability in particular in this respect, provided another reason for its success in the direct fire support role over the jungles of Vietnam.

Tandem seating for the crew of two provided a maximum all-round field of view for the pilot and co-pilot/forward gunner, another advantage that helicopters had over the fixed-wing strike aircraft and gunships when supporting troops on the ground. If the Viet Cong opened fire from their jungle lairs, they were apt to lose the advantage of cover and concealment, and a corollary to this advantage of spotting and firing on the enemy was the ability to spot 'own troops' and to place supporting bursts of machine-gun fire just a few yards from them.

In normal operation, the co-pilot/gunner controlled and fired the

An AH-1G 'HueyCobra' of the 334th Armed Helicopter Company, 12th Combat Aviation Group, III Field Force Vietnam, takes off on a combat support mission in 1969.

Pilots of 'HueyCobra' gunships refuel their helicopters after returning from an operation with the 101st Airborne Division near Fire Base 'Victory' about 12 miles south of the Demilitarized Zone (DMZ) in October 1969.

turret armament, using a hand-held, pantograph-mounted sight to which the turret was slaved. The gunner's field of fire was 230 degrees, ie 115 degrees right and left of the aircraft's centreline, and the turreted weapons could be depressed 50 degrees and elevated 25 degrees. In addition, the gunner had the capability of firing the wing stores. The pilot could only fire the turreted weapons when in the stowed position (the dead ahead turret returned to the stowed position automatically when the gunner released his grip on the slewing switch) but he usually fired the wing stores, utilizing the XM-73 adjustable rocket sight. Rockets were fired in pairs, one rocket from each opposing wing station; any desired number of pairs from one to nineteen could be

In 1970, repairmen work on the electrical switching mechanism of the 40 mm XM-129 grenade launcher fitted to an AH-1G 'Cobra' gunship.

pre-selected on the cockpit-mounted intervalometer. The inboard wing stores were equipped to fire either the XM-18 or XM-18E1 minigun pod, and all wing stores were totally jettisonable.

Two rates of fire were provided for the TAT-102A and XM-28 miniguns, namely 1,600 and 4,000 rounds per minute. The lower rate was for searching or registry fire, while the higher rate was used for attack, the rate of fire being controlled by the gunner's trigger. The XM-129 fired at a single rate of 400 rounds per minute, while the M-61A1 20 mm Vulcan gun fired at a rate of 750 rounds per minute.

In 1969, an XM-35 20 mm cannon kit was added to the weapons available for the AH-1G; six aircraft were equipped and delivered to the US Army in December of that year. A total of 350 of these kits was ordered by the Army; designed jointly by Bell and General Electric, the XM-35 subsystem consisted of a six-barrel, 20 mm automatic cannon, two ammunition boxes and certain structural and electrical modifications. Mounted on the inboard stores attachment of the port stub-wing, the XM-35 had a firing rate of 750 rounds per minute, and the two ammunition boxes, faired flush to the fuselage below the stub-wings, held 1,000 rounds. The total installed weight of the system was 1,172 lbs (532 kg). The crew were protected by seats and side panels made of NOROC armour, manufactured by the Norton Company, and other similar panels protected vital areas of the aircraft.

The Cobra proved to be the prime weapon in the 1971 attack on the North Vietnamese sanctuaries and infiltration routes in Laos, code-named Lamson 719. In this important operation, which took place between 8 February and 9 April, the ARVN I Corps,

An armourer loads a 2.75 in rocket into its pod mounted on an AH-1G 'Cobra' gunship in 1970.

comprising the 1st Infantry Divison, 1st Airborne Division, three battalions of Rangers and three cavalry squadrons, was supported by the following US elements — the 2nd Squadron, the 17th Cavalry with four Air Cavalry troops, the 101st Aviation Group with a number of aviation units under their operational control from the 1st Aviation Brigade, and one squadron of Marine medium transport helicopters.

As an example of the firepower available at the time, the standard armament of the Cobra now included the 2.75 in rocket with a 17 lb warhead, the very effective 2.75 in Flechette rocket and the SX-35 20 mm cannon. The firepower of the division was also enhanced by the intelligence gathering capability of the Seismic intrusion devices, which were dropped by UH-1H helicopters along known infiltration routes. Once enemy movement had been detected, a small unit was lifted into the area ahead of the enemy's determined course of movement and established an effective ambush with artillery and gunships standing by.

Air Cavalry performed two principal missions during Lamson 719 — reconnaissance on the flanks and front of ground operations, and reconnaissance and security of landing zones — but as the campaign progressed the gunships were much in demand by the South Vietnamese units for close fire support. Army UH-1C helicopters were recalled to duty, but the AH-1Cs, which could fly twice as fast as the UH-1H (see page 51) were preferred. In fact, during Lamson 719 the Air Cavalry was used more often in the close fire support than the reconnaissance role, and during the campaign engaged enemy tanks for the first time. Upon sighting a tank or group of tanks, the Cavalry gunships would engage them to maintain contact, then normally turn the target over to the Air Force and continue reconnaissance missions. If tactical aircraft were not available, the gunships would engage tanks until their ordnance was expended, but the choppers would rarely have enough ordnance to destroy every tank in a particular sighting.

Between 8 February and 24 March 1971, the Cavalry sighted 66 tanks, destroying six and immobilizing eight. Three of the destroyed tanks were hit with Flechettes, high explosive and white phosphorous, while the others were destroyed by combinations of Flechettes, high explosive, white phosphorous and high explosive antitank. In turn, the PT-76s' 12.7 mm guns did inflict damage on the Cobras but did not succeed in shooting one down (the PT-76 was better described as a lightly armoured gun carriage than a tank). The Cavalry troops also encountered the Russian Second World War T-34 tanks, but did not engage them.

Summing up Lamson 719, *Newsweek*, although acknowledging that the airmen had flown through some of the heaviest flak of the

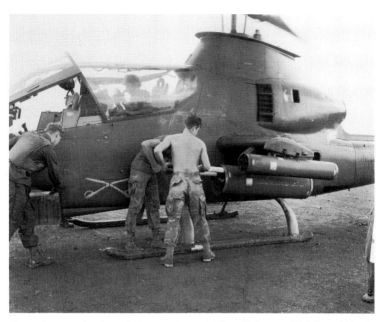

Ground crew load rockets on to a 101st Airborne Division AH-1G 'HueyCobra' in 1973.

Vietnam War, stated in a rather cavalier manner that '. . . the plunge into Laos has been something like an old-time cavalry charge on horseback; admirably heroic, stunningly effective — and terribly costly . . . Despite the risks, it was inevitable that US helicopters should be deeply involved in the Laotian campaign, for more than any other artifact of war, the chopper has become the indelible symbol of the Indochina conflict. Helicopter pilots were among the first Americans killed in the war a decade ago and, under President Nixon's Vietnamization program, they will probably be among the last to leave. In the years between, the chopper's mobility and firepower have added a radically new dimension to warfare . . .'

Whoever may be adjudged the victor in Lamson 719, the ARVN with the help of US air cover — B-52 strikes, fixed-wing strike aircraft and gunships, and helicopter gunships — dealt a crippling blow on the Viet Cong and North Vietnam Army. Reports on supplies and equipment destroyed or captured included over 4,000 individual weapons, more than 1,500 crew-served weapons, 20,000 tons of ammunition, 12,000 tons of rice, 105 tanks, 76 artillery pieces and 405 trucks. Combined air-ground operations resulted in a reported total of 13,914 enemy killed in action.

The US Marine Corps interest in the HueyCobra was

maintained, and in 1969 the Army supplied 38 AH-1Gs to the USMC for training and combat purposes. However, the Marines did not like certain aspects of the AH-1G and insisted on several major modifications. Since they spent much of their time flying over water, they wanted twin engines instead of the AH-1G's single engine. They also argued successfully for the replacement of the 7.62 mm gun system by a 20 mm cannon, and stipulated an improved rotor brake, which was necessary when operating under pressure from the cramped confines of amphibious support ships. The result was the AH-1J (SeaCobra) which made its maiden flight in December 1969.

The decision to use a non-US engine — the T400-CP-400 of the United Aircraft of Canada (later Pratt & Whitney, Canada) — raised a few eyebrows in Washington, but the Canadian contender survived a competitive evaluation test ordered by Secretary of Defense Robert S. McNamara. The AH-1J was submitted to exhaustive testing both by Bell and the USMC, and was approved by the Board of Inspection and Survey (BIS) after trials with the Naval Air Test Center at Patuxent River, Maryland; seven were delivered to VMO-1 at New River in September 1970.

The New River AH-1Js were used for crew and maintenance training tasks, and plans were also afoot to introduce the Marines in Vietnam to the refurbished Huey. Four SeaCobras were subsequently shipped to the war zone aboard Military Airlift Command Douglas C-133 Cargomasters in mid-February 1971. Following re-assembly, the four helicopters were turned over to HML-367, which staged the first combat sortie from its base at Marble Mountain on 22 February. This was the start of an intensive evaluation which lasted slightly over two months and during which the emphasis was on a comparison between the merits of the 7.62 mm and 20 mm gun systems.

The weaponry finally chosen was the electrically operated General Electric turret containing an XM197 three-barrelled 20 mm cannon, which, with its long (5 ft/1.52 m) barrel protruding beneath the nose of the aircraft, was a feature that made the SeaCobra more easily recognizable. Its barrel length dictated that the gun be stowed in the dead ahead position before ordnance carried on the stub-wings could be employed. Essentially a lightweight model of the widely used M-60 cannon, the gun came complete with 750 rounds of ammunition housed in a fuselage-mounted drum, and was nominally capable of achieving a firing rate of 750 rounds per minute. However, it was prone to jamming when overheated, so bursts were confined to 16 shells. The arc of fire was 110 degrees to both left and right of the centreline, with 18 degrees elevation and 50 degrees depression.

In terms of external loads, the SeaCobra was similarly equipped to the HueyCobra, being able to operate with a maximum of four LAU-61 or LAU-68 pods holding 7 and 19 2.75 in rockets respectively. Alternatively, SUU-11A minigun pods could be fitted to the inboard stations or smoke grenade dispensers to the outboard stations, and the total external payload was around 2,200 lbs (99.79 kg). Three primary armaments systems were in operation, and, like the UH-1G, the pilot and co-pilot handled both flight and fire control systems, but the individual duties were not so strictly defined in the SeaCobra. Fuel was sacrificed for payload: the 'basic' rig enabled the SeaCobra to stay in the air for almost two hours, the 'medium' rig just one hour, and the 'heavy' rig only 11 minutes.

In basic terms, the missions assigned to Marine SeaCobras differed little from those of the Army equivalents. The helicopters were specifically tasked with the delivery of weapons fire, search and target acquisition, reconnaissance by fire, multiple weapons fire-support and troop-carrying helicopter support. There was a big difference, however, in relation to the operating bases. The AH-1J was expected to be equally at home on prepared and unprepared surfaces, as well as aboard ships in coastal waters; the result was that the SeaCobra was a rather different bird from the HueyCobra, but there was a certain family resemblance.

BELL UH-1 IROQUOIS

(UH-1A, UH-1B, UH-1C, UH-1D, UH-1E, UH-1H)

Origin Bell Aerospace Corporation, Buffalo 5, New York; **Mission** General purpose helicopter; **Service** US Army.

UH-1A IROQUOIS

Engine T53-L-1A 860 shp shaft-turbine; **Rotor diameter** 43 ft 9 in (13.31 m); **Overall length** 52 ft 10 in (16.07 m); **Skid track** 7 ft 10 in (2.37 m); **Overall height** 14 ft 7 in (4.43 m); **Weight** (empty) 4,020 lbs (1,823 kg), (loaded) 9,195 lbs (4,165 kg); **Maximum speed** (loaded, at sea level) 120 mph (193 km/h); **Cruising speed** (loaded) 106 mph (170 km/h); **Range** (loaded, with reserves) 230 miles (370 km); **Armament** Dependent on role – see below; **Accommodation** Crew of two/four with six passengers, or three stretcher cases, or cargo.

UH-1B IROQUOIS

Engine T53-L-5 1,100 shp shaft-turbine; **Rotor diameter** 44 ft (13.39 m); **Overall length** 53 ft 11 in (16.41 m); **Skid track** 7 ft 10 in (2.37 m); **Overall height** 14 ft 7 in (4.43 m); **Weight** (empty) 4,502 lbs (2,042 kg), (loaded) 11,206 lbs (5,083 kg); **Maximum speed** (loaded, at sea level) 138 mph (222 km/h); **Cruising speed** (loaded) 126 mph (202 km/h); **Range** (loaded, with reserves) 253 miles (407 km); **Armament** Dependent on role – see below; **Accommodation** Two/four crew with eight passengers, or three stretcher cases, or cargo.

The weapons system of the UH-1A, the first version of the Huey helicopter.

UH-1C IROQUOIS

Engine T53-L-11 1,100 shp shaft-turbine; **Rotor diameter** 44 ft (13.39 m); **Overall length** 53 ft (16.13 m); **Skid track** 7 ft 10 in (2.37 m); **Overall height** 14 ft 7 in (4.43 m); **Weight** (empty) 4,830 lbs (2,190 kg), (loaded) 13,330 lbs (6,046 kg); **Maximum speed** (loaded, at sea level) 148 mph (238 km/h); **Cruising speed** (loaded) 136 mph (219 km/h); **Range** (loaded, with reserves) 270 miles (434 km); **Armament** Dependent on role – see below; **Accommodation** Two crew and seven troops or cargo.

UH-1D IROQUOIS

Engine T53-L-11 1,100 shp shaft-turbine; **Rotor diameter** 48 ft 3 in (14.68 m); **Overall length** 57 ft 1 in (17.37 m); **Skid track** 7 ft 10 in (2.37 m); **Overall height** 14 ft 7 in (4.43 m); **Weight** (empty) 4,900 lbs (2,222 kg), (loaded) 8,500 lbs (3,855 kg); **Maximum speed** (loaded, at sea level) 148 mph (238 km/h); **Cruising speed** (loaded) 130 mph (209 km/h); **Range** (loaded, with reserves) 260 miles (418 km); **Armament** Dependent on role – see below; **Accommodation** Two/four crew and eleven passengers or supplies.

UH-1H IROQUOIS

Technical data as for UH-1D but powered by an Avco Corporation T53-L-13 1,400 shp shaft-turbine.

The Bell Model 204, US Army designation UH-1 Iroquois, which consisted of a number of marques, was more commonly known by its nickname 'Huey'. The UH-1 was first conceived in 1955 when the Bell company won a US Army competition for the development of a utility helicopter suitable for front-line evacuation of casualties, general utility missions and as an instrument trainer. Bell gave their winning design the model number 204, but it was known in its production form as the UH-1 (formerly HU-1). It had a Lycoming T53 series shaft-turbine engine capable of running on a wide variety of fuels, and was designed for a minimum of 1,000 hours of operation between overhauls.

The UH-1A was developed from the X-40 prototype, of which three were produced and the first of which flew for the first time on 22 October 1956. The X-40 was followed by six service test models (YH-40) and nine pre-production models (UH-2). The first UH-1As were delivered to the US Army on 30 June 1959 and the last in March 1961; 54 remained in the Army inventory in 1971. Fourteen UH-1As were delivered for use as helicopter instrument trainers with dual controls and instrumentation, together with a device for simulated instrument instruction.

Little is specifically recorded about the UH-1A's performance in the Vietnam conflict, but it was both present and active in the early months of the 'advisory years'. Its mission was the transportation of personnel, casualties and equipment, and as a training aircraft

*US Army UH-1B helicopters recently unloaded from an American freight-
er are still 'dressed' in their protective covering for the ocean voyage.*

for South Vietnamese crews. It could carry a payload of 2,175 lbs
(986 kg) and an external cargo of 3,000 lbs (1,360 kg).

A top priority in those early days was for a satisfactory aircraft for
medical operation. As early as 1953, the Aviation Section of the
Surgeon General's Office had specified the desirable characteristics of an Army air ambulance. It was to be highly manoeuvrable for
use in combat zones, of low profile, and capable of landing in a
small area. It was to carry a crew of four and at least four stretcher
patients, yet be easily loaded with litters by just two people. It had
to be able to hover with a full casualty load even in high altitude
areas, and to cruise at about 130 mph (209 km/h) fully loaded.

In 1962, the Army's basic utility aircraft, the UH-1B, still did not
meet these standards. It was, however, a small craft with a low
profile, and those who flew it could console themselves with the
fact that the Huey was a far better air ambulance than the one their
predecessors had flown in the Korean War ten years before. It had
nearly twice the speed and endurance of the H-13 Sioux, and
could carry patients inside the aircraft, allowing a medical orderly to
administer in-flight treatment.

Although the 'A' and 'B' model Huey engines often lacked
enough power to work in the heat and high altitudes of South
Vietnam, they were much stronger than earlier Army helicopter
engines. A great advance in helicopter propulsion had come in the
1950s with the adaptation of the gas turbine engine to helicopter
flight. The piston-drive engines used in Korea and on the UH-34
utility helicopters in the 1950s and early 1960s had produced only

one horsepower for each three pounds of engine weight, but the gas turbines installed on the UH-1 Hueys had a much more favourable efficiency ratio.

This development permitted the construction of a small, low-profile aircraft that was still large enough to carry a crew of four and three stretcher patients against the back wall of the cabin. The critical factor in planning all helicopter flights with heavy cargoes is what pilots know as the 'density altitude' — the effective height above sea level computed on the basis of the actual altitude and the air temperature. The warmer the air, the less its resistance to the rotor blades and the less lift they produce. In the high-density altitudes encountered in II Corps Zone, UH-1A and UH-1B Hueys with a full crew — pilot, aircraft commander, crew chief, and medical orderly — often could carry no more than two patients at a time.

During three military operations against the Viet Cong in War Zone D from November 1962 to March 1963, the South Vietnamese Army and the Americans were acutely aware of the problem of evacuating the wounded. The thick jungle in the area made resupply and medical evacuation by helicopter extremely difficult, and some of the South Vietnamese units carried their wounded for as long as four days before finding a suitable landing area for the UH-1As. Some means was needed of hoisting the wounded — or anyone who needed rescuing — from terrain over which helicopters could hover but not land upon.

Two rather impractical pick-up systems were tried and discarded; one involved a collapsible box-like platform which the ground troops had to strap to the upper reaches of a tree, while the

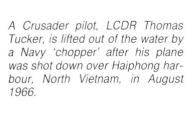

A Crusader pilot, LCDR Thomas Tucker, is lifted out of the water by a Navy 'chopper' after his plane was shot down over Haiphong harbour, North Vietnam, in August 1966.

Steel netting is used to make a helicopter platform on the matted surface of tall trees. This arrangement was considered too dangerous for medical evacuation in Vietnam.

A wounded paratrooper of the 101st Airborne Division is lifted from jungle terrain to a 'dust-off' medical helicopter in Ninh Thuan Province, 1967.

other scheme used two stainless steel nets and a large platform which were dropped on to the 'jungle canopy'. The disadvantages of these rejected 'Jungle Canopy Platform Systems' were numerous. With the first, the box-like contraption had first to be dropped to the ground and retrieved by the ground troops, who had then to clamber up a tall tree to fix the platform in position before hauling up the wounded! The second idea involved the hovering helicopter unrolling the two steel nets on the matted jungle tree tops so that they intersected at midpoint; the platform upon which the helicopter actually landed was then lowered on top. The 1st Cavalry Division tried out these rescue devices in non-combat conditions, but no unit would risk using them in a real firefight.

However, the Army did develop a piece of supplemental equipment for the Huey that both advanced the art of medical evacuation and placed extraordinary new demands on air ambulance pilots: the personnel rescue hoist. The hoist was a winch mounted on a support that was anchored to the floor and roof of the helicopter cabin, usually just inside the starboard side door behind the pilot's seat. When the door was open, the hoist could be rotated on its support to position its cable and pulleys outside the aircraft, clear of the skids, so that the cable could be lowered to and raised from the ground. After a UH-1 was outfitted with the necessary electrical system, the aircraft crew could quickly install or remove the hoist.

On a hoist mission, while the aircraft hovered, the medical orderly or crew chief would use the hoist cable to lower any one of several types of stretchers or harnesses to casualties below. If a wounded soldier and his comrades could not handle the apparatus, the crew chief would sometimes lower the medic with the device; the hoist would then raise both the medic and the casualty to the helicopter. The standard hoist eventually installed in the UH-1D and UH-1H Hueys could lift up to 600 lbs (272 kg) in one load and could lower a harness or stretcher about 250 feet (76 m) below the aircraft. The hoist system was not, however, operational in Vietnam until May 1966.

The first small unit of UH-1s had arrived in Vietnam during the autumn of 1962 under the designation Utility Tactical Transport Helicopter Company (UTTCO). The unit comprised 15 model UH-1As which were outfitted to test a variety of missions. All the helicopters had been fitted with armament that comprised 2.75 in rockets (16 mounted eight to a side on the helicopter's skids rather than pod mounted) and two .30 calibre Browning air-cooled machine-guns, which were also mounted on the skids but near to the large cargo doors where they could be reloaded by crewmen.

The Hueys were relatively small choppers; their assignment to

A flight of UH-1B helicopters viewed from the cockpit of one of them as they participate in a mission against the Viet Cong north of Bien Hoa in 1967.

Tan Son Nhut was most welcome and they were soon flying escort to the H-21 Shawnees.

Taking advantage of their small size, the Hueys could zip in and out of the ponderous Shawnee formations, laying down suppressive fire and attacking any target that appeared to be hostile with a withering blast of rocket and machine-gun fire. The Viet Cong initially recoiled at this sudden onslaught of new American technology but quickly responded by blasting away at the helicopters with heavier automatic weapons and attempting to evade the attackers whenever possible. The Hueys, however, could be heard from miles away, their rotors with their loud thumping noise warning the enemy of their approach to a target.

UTTCO pilots and crews began to gain considerable confidence in the craft and their mission, and Government officials quickly began to compile relevant statistics. They were rather impressive: only one UH-1A gunship had been knocked down in five months of combat flying (although several others had been damaged in the 1,800 hours of combat missions); the H-21 loss had dropped by 25 per cent when escorted by gunships, while during the same period the loss rate for unescorted troop helicopters had risen by

UH-1Bs of the US Army Support Command, Vietnam, approach a landing area at Song Be in 1967 to pick up Vietnamese troops from a besieged landing zone.

nearly double; an estimated 250 Viet Cong had been killed.

The UTTCO crews took a severe blow to their prestige, however, when on 2 January 1963 the South Vietnamese decided to mount the raid on Ap Bac. Although the raid, which is briefly described in the H-21 Shawnee section (see page 144), was judged to be a success, a number of serious lessons were learned from the event. Ten H-21s were being supported by five Huey gunships, and as they thundered into the landing zone they were met by a well-organized and determined enemy. The VC had built mortar and heavy machine-gun emplacements and greeted the helicopters with a withering blast of fire. The combined weapons quickly took their toll and four H-21s were destroyed while the Hueys buzzed around like angry hornets trying to protect their charges. The armament of the gunships was simply not enough to dislodge the enemy and the mission had been planned without any form of fixed-wing support, so by the time fighter-bombers had been scrambled into the area, one of the Hueys had been knocked down. Although the enemy began to disperse into the forest in the face of the 'heavy metal' air strike, it is highly likely that with the damage and casualties they had inflicted the Viet Cong considered they had won the day.

The main lesson to be learned from the battle of Ap Bac was that even heavily armed gunships simply could not destroy an entrenched and resourceful enemy who was prepared to take heavy losses defending his turf, and fixed-wing air strikes would have to be incorporated into any form of airmobile operation where the enemy was suspected of being dug in. The weakness of the H-21 was highlighted, the shattered machines in the landing zone around Ap Bac proving the mute truth that the day of the 'Flying Banana' was coming to an end.

By June of 1963, most of the light helicopter companies had phased in the new UH-1B helicopters and had transferred their aviators, ground staff and crew chiefs to the new aircraft. However, it would not be until 27 June 1964 that the last H-21 Shawnee was formally retired by the US Army Support Command, Vietnam. By this time, the UH-1B Huey troop transports had emerged from the Bell production line to replace the H-21, and by the end of 1964 nearly 300 Huey 'slicks' (troop carriers) were operating in South Vietnam. Their mission was described by the US Army as 'transport of personnel, equipment, supplies, and to serve as an aerial weapons platform'. ('Personnel' may be defined here as armed troops or casualties.)

A development of the original UH-1A, the helicopter initially had a 960 shp Lycoming T53-L-5 shaft-turbine, then it was uprated to a 1,100 shp T53-L-11 shaft-turbine. The UH-1B, with its more powerful, lightweight engine, had some power to spare as compared with the 1A. It could hover and take off with ten passengers and a crew of two, and was also quieter, started more easily, and was simpler to maintain.

An Army training film shown to pilot candidates flying UH-1Bs at Fort Rucker boasted that the T53-L-11 gas-turbine engine developed 1,100 horsepower yet weighed only 500 lbs (226 kg). The film went on to explain that a turbine is basically a jet engine with a fan placed in the exhaust. An animation then showed an engine cutaway illustrating the 12 in (30 cm) diameter turbine fan spinning in the gas behind the jet engine. This single turbine fan was connected by a shaft running back through the engine to the transmission. The pressure of the gases pushing through this fan generated sufficient force to turn the single 44 ft (13.39 m) rotor system and the 8 ft (2.43 m) tail rotor assembly and lift the 4,500 lb (2041 kg) machine together with a load of 6,700 lbs (3039 kg) into the air.

The animation then dissolved to a Huey banking away to swoop down on a jungle, followed by a view of the helicopter sitting in a clearing before rising vertically. The announcer said at this point, 'Though not recommended, the Huey is capable of hovering vertically up to an altitude of 10,000 feet on a standard day'. The film then went on to show how the UH-1B was variously configured as an air ambulance (nicknamed 'Medevac' or 'Dust-Off') carrying a pilot, co-pilot, crew chief, medical orderly and three stretchers; as a gunship ('Guns') lifting pilot, co-pilot and two gunners, one of whom was the crew chief; operating machine-guns, rockets, or grenade launchers; and as a troop carrier ('Slick') with space for eight soldiers and two crew-operated door guns.

After some experimentation, it was decided to deploy the helicopters in what, from the ground, looked like rough 'V' formations. The choppers would fly in the stepped 'V' configuration, taking care and keeping distance to avoid turbulence from each other's large rotors. Escorts would fly slightly ahead of, to the side and to the rear of the 'slicks', and would arrive over the target area a few minutes before the troop carriers and open fire to soften up the area and attack clearly identified enemy targets.

Keeping the landing zone protected was of prime importance, and if the LZ was on firm ground and lacking obstacles the Americans felt that a twelve-Huey 'slick' formation could unload their troops and be back in the air within two minutes, minimizing the helicopters' exposure to enemy fire. Like most other theories in the Vietnam War, the two-minute interval proved to be wildly optimistic and was possibly only feasible in the most ideal of conditions; the amount and accuracy of enemy fire obviously also posed a threat to the two-minute notion. Other factors also had to be considered, the most important being the surface of the LZ. If it happened to be a rice paddy or an area with an unstable ground mass, the helicopters would go into a hover as low as possible from the ground while the troops made the best of jumping overboard. The hovering not only increased the time of operation but the additional height also made the 'slicks' better targets, although the fixed-wing element assisted greatly in enforcing safety on the landing zone.

The ideal battlefield situation was to have all the 'slicks' land and take off *together*. The mass envelopment of the helicopters distracted enemy fire from concentrating on one particular machine and also permitted the landing of a massed body of airborne soldiers who would soon be firing into the enemy positions. However, the landing phase was not easy to accomplish for several reasons. The noise from a combined number of 'slicks' was extremely loud and the landing 'V' patterns could be disrupted if VC fire was accurate. Landing simultaneously was made more difficult because of the stepped altitude of the formation, the rotor wash encountered during the descent and the uncertainty of finding a suitable touchdown spot for each of the ships. In practice,

A Vietnamese Army medic arrives at the Chi Lang Training Center, a staging area for an assault operation on a Viet Cong stronghold on a nearby mountain. About 70 aircraft were used including Huey gunships and troop-carrying 'slicks', Caribous and light observation planes. B-52 bombers paved the way for the successful mission, on 17 February 1966.

no terrain in areas of combat provided absolutely ideal conditions for landing. In the Mekong Delta, water was sometimes chest deep and rather than maintaining a lower hover and risk drowning the troops, the ship was held with its skids just under the water level. In jungle areas, grass 10-12 ft (3-3.6 m) high was also encountered. The two-minute landing intervals, even assuming it was achieved, nevertheless seemed like eternity for the crews.

The armed UH-1B Huey gunships along with the 'slicks' saw much action in the service of the 'Air Cav'. During 1966, the Army developed its gunship helicopter programme which saw a platoon of gunships (eight UH-1Bs) assigned as an element of a helicopter assault company. This plan gave the company instant protection which could be relied upon to protect troop helicopters during landing and take-off from a landing zone. Of the eight ships in each platoon, five were kept at operational readiness while the remaining three were undergoing servicing and maintenance or being held in reserve. When sent into action, the Hueys would fly in two pairs called light fire teams while the fifth helicopter could

Above *This UH-1B helicopter, located at Tan Son Nhut Air Base in 1967, is armed with two sets of the LAW 54/A rocket launchers and an M-79 grenade.*

Below *A Navy UH-1B dives into the attack over an area of thick brush in 1967.*

Above *A naval gunner fires a .30 calibre machine-gun from a Navy UH-1B over the Mekong Delta in 1967.*

Below *Aviation Ordnanceman Michael Draper places a 2.75-in rocket in the rocket tubes of a US Navy UH-1B helicopter aboard USS* Harnett County *(LST-821).*

join one of the teams when needed.

The gunships were called upon to do hazardous work and the Huey's relatively low speed and less than snappy manoeuvrability made it a good target for the enemy. However, it could sting back hard and often. Various armament systems could be installed in and on the helicopter. The UH-1B was armed with four 7.62 mm M-60 machine-guns, a 40 mm grenade launcher, 48 2.75 in rockets and an M22 guided missile. The XM3 armament system boasted two rocket pods (one on each side of the Huey), each of which could hold 24 unguided 2.75 in folding fin rockets, while the XM16 armament included two rocket pods, also located one on each side of the Huey and each holding seven unguided 2.75 in folding fin rockets. Two M-60 machine-guns were provided for the door gunners, and there were also two flexguns, externally mounted M-60CAI 7.62 mm machine-guns. The standard M-60 rate of fire (2,400 rounds per minute) had been uprated in the M-60CAI to 4,000 rpm, but they were restricted to a three-second maximum firing time with a momentary automatic stop between firings. To feed the weapons, twelve feeder ammunition boxes were located in the cargo compartment, as used by the troop transport. The rockets could be fired in a combination of ways: singly, in pairs, or in massive salvos from the pods.

A few UH-1Bs were fitted with the French SS-11 missile system. This system, which employed a wire-guided armour-piercing missile, had been used in Vietnam since the arrival of the 1st Cavalry Division, but the lack of lucrative targets had reduced its usefulness. The system had been standardized in the US Army since 1960 when it replaced the lighter French SS-10 missile, and since then hundreds of gunners had been trained at Fort Rucker in the use of the SS-11. Hueys mounting the SS-11 were alerted in April 1968 when NVA PT-76 tanks were sighted in the Lang Vei area during the enemy attack on the Special Forces camp, but no missiles were used on that occasion.

Although the Huey was an Army helicopter, some UH-1Bs were loaned to the US Navy for service with the riverine fleet and the insertion of the Navy's Sea-Air-Land (SEAL) commando teams. The fleet's airmobility for lifting ammunition and supplies from the US Seventh Fleet's logistic ships to the combatants on station was provided by the UH-34 Seahorse, CH-46 Sea Knight and CH-53 Sea Stallion, handled by Marine units. Ship-based helicopters such as the SH-3 Sea King and UH-2 Seasprite were the key components of the search and rescue (SAR) system established to retrieve downed enemy flyers both at sea and in enemy territory, but at the beginning of the Vietnam War the Navy lacked a gunship.

It therefore requested helicopters to protect and assist the river

Left *Three members of a US Navy Seal Team descend from a hovering Huey by rapelling down ropes to set up an ambush position.*

Right *A UH-1B of Light Helicopter Attack Squadron 3 flies over the Mekong Delta in 1968.*

Below right *South Vietnamese Marines wait to board a Huey helicopter after an operation in the Mekong Delta in November 1967.*

Below *An armed UH-1B Iroquois lifts off from the flight deck of USS* Hunterdon County *(LST-838) in support of riverine operations in the Mekong Delta.*

Above *A US Navy UH-1B comes in to land aboard the Tank Landing Ship USS* Garnett County *(LST-786) while she is anchored in the Co Chien River to provide support for Operation 'Game Warden' forces in January 1970.*

Below *A crew chief demonstrates to a comrade the proper way to load and arm aerial rockets on a UH-1B helicopter in November 1967.*

Above *A Navy airman flying a US Navy UH-1B fires his twin .30-calibre machine-gun at VC positions in the Mekong Delta in November 1967.*

Below *In November 1972, an officer loads a TOW missile as another officer stands by. This TOW Anti-Tank Missile System mounted on a UH-1B helicopter is operated by the 12th Combat Air Group located at Bien Hoa Air Force Base.*

Above *An artilleryman of the 23rd (Americal) Infantry Division guides in a UH-1D helicopter bringing men and supplies for a new fire base, January 1970.*

Below *An Air Cavalry officer boards a UH-1D Huey for an aerial reconnaissance mission over the National Forest Reserve south of Quang Tri in August 1968.*

patrol boats (PBR) and air-cushion vehicles (PACV) operating under the auspices of 'Game Warden' (Task Force 116) in the Mekong Delta. Eight UH-1Bs were initially supplied and SAR crews were borrowed to fly them, and this small force of helicopters and personnel was split into four detachments. Each detachment was assigned two of the ex-Army UH-1Bs, eight crewmen, and eight pilots, and each detachment was given a number. The first unit, Detachment 29, reported for training by Army instructors at Vung Tau during July 1966, and during the five week course the Navy pilots were taught to handle and maintain the Huey. Army combat instructors tutored the Navy pilots on what they felt would be the best combat tactics to employ during operations over the Delta, and trained them on the types of weapons which would be used on the river patrols. Maps, of course, were available, but the Navy pilots were at first dismayed when they saw the complexity of the 3,000 miles of navigable waterways over which they would be operating.

The new detachments, which assumed the full title of HC-1 Detachment Vung Tau, were assigned water-borne bases in the

Men of the 101st Airborne Division move away from UH-1D helicopters on the second wave of the assault on Vung Ro Bay during Operation 'John Paul Jones' in July 1966.

Pilot and co-pilot weapons and survival gear, consisting of individual survival packs and M-16 rifles, aboard a UH-1D helicopter.

form of the modified dock landing ships USS *Tortuga* (LSD-26) and USS *Comstock* (LSD-19). Operational missions began in the middle of September when the Hueys started patrolling from the *Tortuga* as the River Patrol Force. The Army instructors took a liking to their Navy comrades-in-arms and gave them the name 'Seawolves'; the bluejackets in turn liked the image it portrayed and picked up much glory in the American press as the war progressed.

On 1 April 1967, the Navy activated Helicopter Attack (Light) Squadron (HAL 3) at Vung Tau to assume the overall responsibility for Task Force 116 with aerial fire support, observation and medical evacuation. By September 1968, the 421-man Seawolves squadron controlled detachments of two helicopters each at five shore bases and on board three converted tank landing ships (LST) stationed in the large rivers of the Mekong Delta. In 1969, HAL 3's Huey strength stood at 33 which now included UH-1Cs.

The SEALs were nowhere more active than in the Rung Sat Special Zone, a treacherous and disease-infected mangrove swamp surrounding the shipping channel to Saigon; those assigned to this area operated out of Nha Bhe as Detachment Golf. These elite naval units normally formed six-man squads carrying out day and night ambushes, hit-and-run raids, reconnaissance patrols, salvage dives and special intelligence operations. They used landing craft, SEAL team assault boats (STAB), armoured trimarans, PBRs or 'slicks' for transportation to and from their target areas. In swampland such as the Rung Sat, the SEALs could be lowered and picked up by a hovering 'slick' using ropes.

In September 1965, Bell introduced the Model 540 'door hinge' rotor, with a blade width of 27 in (68 cm). This developed version of the UH-1B, named the UH-1C, offered some increase in speed and manoeuvrability over its predecessor, and also carried a heavier payload. The transition from the 1B to the 1D has been described as an 'awkward pause with the original "C" design'. The principal assignment of the UH-1 from the 1B onwards in the armed escort role was to protect the Boeing-Vertol CH-47 Chinook medium transport helicopter, but there was a critical stage in the Huey programme when the technicians insisted that the US Army should not go beyond the UH-1B model with Bell, and that there should be a new tactical transport 'between' the Huey and medium transport helicopter. A rearguard action was fought with the Pentagon to keep the Huey programme viable, and, when the most realistic size of the Chinook became apparent, it was decided to go straight for the UH-1D. By thus resolutely pushing for the Huey and a larger-sized Chinook, the US Army accelerated its airmobility programme by years. The UH-1C's mission had been officially described as transporting personnel, special teams or crews, equipment and supplies; medical evacuation; ambulance service; reconnaissance and security; point target and area fire by attachment of appropriate weapons; and instrument trainer. Mention is made of using the 'older armed UH-1Cs' during the Tet Offensive in 1968 and 290 were still in the Army inventory in 1971.

The redesignated Bell Model 205, christened by the Army the UH-1D, had increased power rating and fuel capacity as compared with the UH-1B, and relocation of the fuel cells provided more cabin space. The Huey UH-1D was first tested by the 11th Air Assault Division at Fort Benning in August 1963, and examples fitted with new armoured seats for the pilots accompanied the 1st Cavalry Division to Vietnam.

The increased cabin space and longer fuselage of the UH-1D over the UH-1B permitted the 'Dust-Off' crews to accommodate six stretcher patients or nine 'walking wounded'. The longer rotor blade also gave this chopper more lifting power, but the high-density altitudes of the two northern corps zones, where US infantry troops did most of their fighting, still prevented the Medevac pilots from making full use of the aircraft's carrying capacity. Finally, in 1967 the commander of the 4th Infantry Division complained about his aeromedical evacuation support.

The 498th Medical Company, which served the Central Highlands, had performed 100 hoist missions from July 1966 to February 1967 but had aborted three because of mechanical failures of the hoist and nine because of the inability of the UH-1D to hover. Apart from its inadequate engine power potential, the helicopter was burdened with a heavy single sideband (high frequency) radio and navigation system, and the sheer weight of the hoist apparatus itself. Since the crew chief worked on the same side of the aircraft as the hoist, the helicopter was heavily overweighted on one side and a strong gust of wind from the other side could endanger its stability.

In July 1967, the arrival at Long Binh of the 45th Medical Company (Air Ambulance) equipped with new, powerful UH-1Hs (see page 79) marked the end of the Huey's propulsion problem. Tests were conducted on the engine power of the UH-1D, Kaman HH-43 Huskie and the new UH-1H with its Avco Corporation T53-L-13 engine, and the study showed that the maximum load of an aircraft hovering more than about 20 ft (6 m) above the ground (out of ground effect) on a normal 95°F (35°C) day in the western Highlands was 184 lbs (83 kg) for the UH-1D with an L-11 engine, 380 lbs (172 kg) for the Huskie, and 1,063 lbs (482 kg) for the UH-1H with an L-13 engine. By January 1968, all UH-1D air ambulances had been re-allocated as assault troop helicopters.

Meanwhile, both UH-1Bs and 1Ds had been deployed in mid-October 1965 when the 'Air Cav' fought its first major battle. The North Vietnamese Army had begun a major operation in the Central Highlands, and there was every reason to believe that it planned to cut South Vietnam in two. The Communist regulars opened their campaign with an attack on the Pleime Special Forces camp 25 miles (40 km) southwest of Pleiku. General Westmoreland directed the 1st Cavalry Division to seek out and destroy this enemy force consisting of the 32nd, 33rd, and 66th North Vietnamese Army Regiments, and this became the month-long campaign known as the Battle of the Ia Drang Valley.

Initially, the 1st Cavalry reinforced the ARVN in relieving the Pleime Camp, as a result of which the NVA regiments broke contact and disappeared into the jungle. The 1st Brigade of the 1st Cavalry was given the mission of organizing a systematic search for the elusive enemy, and on 1 November some unusual activity was spotted just a few miles from Pleime Camp. The Air Cavalry Squadron seized the opportunity of mounting an attack with most of its rifle and gunship platoons, and killed 78 of the enemy as well as capturing 57 prisoners. In this first skirmish of the Ia Drang Valley campaign, both helicopter crews and troopers were shocked at the almost suicidal short ranges at which they came to grips with the enemy; the bulk of the North Vietnamese attack

SP/5 Zolten Szoke of the 82nd Aviation Battalion, wearing chest armour and a groin protector and holding an M-60 machine-gun, demonstrates the position of the crew chief of a UH-1D helicopter.

force was within thirty paces of the LZ perimeter before it was discovered. During the firefight, emergency medical evacuation zones had to be literally hacked out of the jungle with hand axes. After the Pleime battle, the best estimate was that the major enemy force had moved along the Ia Drang Valley close to the base of the Chu Pong Mountains, so the 1st Cavalry went in pursuit.

On 14 November, the 1st Battalion, 7th Cavalry, commanded by Lieutenant Colonel Harold G. Moore, began the pivotal operation of the Ia Drang campaign and chose landing zone X-Ray for the initial air assault. The lift battalion gunships took up the fire from the fixed-wing strike aircraft and ground artillery towards noon, flying immediately ahead of the troop transport Hueys. An intelligence assessment had suggested correctly that 'eight to ten UH-1Ds could land at one time' but the terrain surrounding the LZ was thick scrub trees and elephant grass.

The major problem in the 1st Battalion's three-day engagement was care of the wounded and medical evacuation. Colonel Moore had this to say about his helicopter support after being relieved on the 16th by the 2nd Battalion, 7th Cavalry: 'I have the highest admiration, praise and respect for the outstanding professionalism and courage of the UH-1D pilots and crews who ran a gauntlet of enemy fire time after time to help us. They never refused to come in; they followed instructions beautifully; they were great. We in

Paratroopers of Co 'B', 2nd Bn(Abn), 327th Infantry, about to make a combat assault from UH-1D helicopters in the Chu Lai area during Operation 'Benton' in 1967.

turn called them in when fire was the lightest and tried to have everything ready for each landing to keep them on the ground a minimum time. None was shot down and destroyed, although most of them took hits. Two aircraft were brought in which did not get out.

'One received enemy fire in the engine and had to land in an open area just off the northern portion of the LZ; the other clipped a few tree tops with the main rotor upon landing in the LZ and had to be left. Crews of both aircraft were immediately lifted out by other helicopters. Both downed helicopters were immediately secured by elements of Company D without orders per battalion SOP — they being the nearest troops. Both were slightly damaged only and were slung out two days later by CH-47 Chinooks. During the three-day battle these were the only two downed helicopters.'

The Ia Drang battle lasted 35 days, and on 26 November 1965 the 1st Cavalry Division had completed its mission of pursuit and destruction. In those 35 days, the aircraft delivered 5,048 tons of cargo from main bases into the hands of troops in the field. In addition, they transported 8,216 tons into Pleiku from various depots (primarily Qui Nhon and Nha Trang). Whole infantry battalions and artillery batteries were moved by air, and

UH-1D helicopters come to Fire Base 'Sabre' to pick up members of the 101st Airborne Division in October 1969.

approximately 2,700 refugees were taken to safety. In all this flying, 59 aircraft were hit by enemy fire — three while on the ground — and only four were shot down, of which three were recovered.

General Westmoreland stated: 'The ability of the Americans to meet and defeat the best troops the enemy could put on the field of battle was once more demonstrated beyond any possible doubt as was the validity of the Army's airmobile concept.'

During the early 1960s, US Marine units in South-east Asia had little to choose from in the way of helicopters except for the Sikorsky UH-34, while it became more than obvious that the US Army had a real winner in the Bell UH-1 Huey series, which was more nimble than the UH-34 and could not only haul troops but could also be easily converted into a gunship with a deadly sting. Accordingly, a competition was carried out to supply the 'leathernecks' with a new helicopter, and no one was surprised when the Bell UH-1 came out a clear winner when the competition results were announced on 3 March 1962.

Consequently, the Department of Defense planned for a new helicopter (to be designated UH-1E) to begin replacing the Kaman OH-43D Huskie — a crash rescue helicopter — and the Cessna

UH-1D helicopters from the 217th Helicopter Company, South Vietnamese Air Force, race above the paddy fields carrying infantrymen towards a landing zone west of Can Tho City in 1970.

O-1B and O-1C fixed-wing forward observation aircraft. The UH-1E was generally very similar to the UH-1B, but had a personnel hoist installed from the start, and the Marines for whom it was intended required a rotor brake and certain special electronics. UH-1Bs were loaned to the Marines for training and the 'leathernecks' were soon proficient at handling the new machine.

Since the Marines must be able to operate off Navy ships, a method of securing the rotor was needed to prevent the large blades from windmilling after landing and thus posing a definite hazard for sailors aboard ship. A rotor brake was thus installed to effectively control the blades. Other important changes included the use of aluminium for construction rather than the earlier magnesium and the addition of radio gear and an electrical system catering for USMC mission requirements. Although aluminium tends to quickly corrode if not properly cared for in a salty environment, it is a much more solid material than magnesium which will virtually disintegrate when exposed to salt.

During the latter part of 1963, operational testing of the UH-1E took place aboard the USS *Guadalcanal*, and the first machine was officially handed over to the Marines during February 1964.

A 'victim' is hoisted aboard a UH-1D Medevac helicopter during a 1970 demonstration of the jungle penetrator.

Helicopters soon began flowing to VMO squadrons, and, after the Gulf of Tonkin Resolution in August when Lyndon B. Johnson ordered strictly controlled air attacks against North Vietnam military targets, more direct action was taken to effectively arm the UH-1Es. A quick-fit kit was devised which would arm the aircraft with two M-60C machine-guns mounted on a rack which normally carried rocket pods, and associated electrical equipment and a gun sight were fitted in the cockpit. Other armaments were also tested including .50 calibre machine-guns and two M-60s mounted in an Emerson nose turret.

During May 1965, armed UH-1Es began to arrive in Vietnam to support Marine ground units. VMO-2 and VMO-6 became operational with the type and were assigned to Marine Air Group 16 and based at Marble Mountain, just west of Danang. Since this was essentially a base 'in the open' without the usual hangar and maintenance shed facilities, the physical fitness of the aircraft, not to mention that of the mechanics working in the sweltering sun and torrential downpours, suffered accordingly. Sand and gravel also posed a hazard to engines and rotor blades; the latter had an estimated life of about 1,000 hours, but operations in the field saw this life span decrease to just 700 hours.

Maintenance was not the only problem. The enemy considered the Marine helicopter units to be a particular thorn in their side and began to plan a devastating attack. In a well-mounted night assault on 27 October 1965, the Viet Cong hit Marble Mountain airbase with rockets, grenades and gun fire, completely destroying 19 helicopters and inflicting substantial damage on 11 others. Marine Air Group 16 suffered particularly heavily, losing 13 of its UH-1Es as completely destroyed while several others were knocked out of action for major repairs. In the space of a couple of hours, MAG-16 was reduced to flying only four UH-1Es.

The Marines were always short of UH-1Es, and only 56 of the type were active by March 1966. Two other VMO squadrons, however, were formed during this period and the Marines had to take twenty UH-1Bs from the Army. These aircraft were used for training, but they had drawbacks including the fact they were not equipped with rotor brakes, making them distinctly unpopular with the deck crews! However, this infusion enabled training UH-1Bs to be assigned to combat units. The UH-1E built up an excellent combat record in Vietnam and the type served until 1973 when the Americans pulled out of the Vietnam War.

Following replacement of the original T53-L-11 shaft-turbine by

A crew chief from the 162nd (Assault Helicopter) Aviation Company prepares to refuel a UH-1D helicopter in 1970.

A member of Co 'B', 2nd Bn, 7th Cavalry, 1st Cavalry Division (Airmobile) guides in a UH-1D helicopter for extraction operations in Phuoc Thanh Province, 1971.

the 1,400 shp T53-L-13, the version of the UH-1D in production in 1967 was redesignated UH-1H. The details for the UH-1H were the same as for the UH-1D, with the exception of the more powerful engine. Initial deliveries began in September 1967 and continued at a steady rate; a contract was placed the same month for 553 aircraft, of which deliveries began in December 1968.

Although the basic overall details were the same, the UH-1H did have other advantages over the UH-1D (which incidentally was the most numerous helicopter in Vietnam) apart from its engine. In the tests at Long Binh referred to on page 72, the UH-1D could not lift a casualty of average weight in those temperature conditions; the UH-1H on the other hand could pull five hoist patients. After the departure in September 1968 of the last UH-1Ds, the entire air ambulance fleet was equipped with UH-1Hs, solving many of the problems caused by high density altitudes, hoist missions and heavy loads.

Also, unlike most of the UH-1Ds, the UH-1H was fully instrumented for flight at night and in poor weather, and proved to be a rugged machine, needing comparatively little time for maintenance and repairs. Like the earlier models, the single-rotor

The UH-1E helicopter was generally similar to the UH-1B but had a personnel hoist installed from the start of its career in Vietnam.

UH-1H came with skids rather than wheels to permit landing on marshy or rough terrain. One disadvantage was that with only two main rotor blades, the loss of part or all of one blade made balance of the propulsion system untenable. Another was that the aircraft had a flammable magnesium-aluminium alloy hull. However, in most respects the UH-1H proved an ideal general purpose helicopter, and in particular an excellent vehicle for combat medical evacuation.

Finally, a few more of the Bell UH-1 Iroquois series featured in the Huey family. In 1969, four UH-1L transport Hueys were acquired to take over the transportation duties of the Seawolves (a secondary task which had been assigned once they had increased their strength, and a task which was detracting from the 'Game Warden' Mekong Delta mission). These Navy machines were utility versions of the UH-1Es assigned to the Marine Corps, and were flight-tested with amphibious landing gear which could be fitted to all Hueys. UH-1Ls also performed well in the 'Sealords' campaign conducted by 'Game Warden' vessels on the waterways abutting the Cambodian border from Oct 1968 to Jan 1969.

A US Navy UH-1E helicopter patrols overhead as boats of the South Vietnamese Navy's River Assault Group (RAG) 22 wind their way up a narrow canal in search of Viet Cong guerrillas. The operational area is located 13 miles south-east of Saigon.

The Department of Defense picked the Bell HH-1K (also similar to the USMC UH-1E) to become the Navy's Search and Rescue Huey, and part of the order placed in 1969 for 27 helicopters was assigned to HAL 3. (In the latter part of 1970, the unit was operating 27 UH-1Bs, two UH-1Cs, four UH-1Ls and two HH-1Ks.) The 'Game Warden' force participated in their Operation 'Tran Hung Dao XI' in 1970, the Navy's term for the American move into Cambodia that, when it became known, caused a furore in the States. Five of HAL 3's detachments saw service in the Cambodian mission and their helicopters were the first US machines to land in Phnom Penh, the Cambodian capital, while the three detachments seeing the heaviest tour of duty (3, 8 and 9) recorded 748 combat missions.

By mid-1970, the Seawolves were being affected by the Nixon policy of 'Vietnamization' — as were other US units — and missions began to carry South Vietnamese military personnel, be they VNAF or ARVN. The Vietnamese had been drawn from their

UH-1H helicopters of the 182nd Aviation Company deploy troops at Fort Bragg, North Carolina. The UH-1H, an updated version of the UH-1D, proved an ideal general purpose helicopter and an excellent vehicle for combat medical evacuation in Vietnam.

own helicopter units and were experienced pilots and gunners. Also, at this time the Seawolves began to receive their first UH-1M Hueys, trading in their older helicopters on a one-to-one basis. The UH-1M was a Hughes Aircraft Iroquois night fighter and was equipped with a night tracker system to detect and acquire ground targets under low ambient lighting conditions. Two sensors mounted on the nose of the cabin served a low-light-level TV system with three cockpit displays and a direct-view system using an image intensifier in the cockpit/gunner's station. Three UH-1Ms were initially deployed by the US Army in early 1970 to evaluate the system.

BOEING-VERTOL CH-46 SEA KNIGHT

(CH-46A, SH-46D; UH-46A, UH-46D)

Origin Boeing-Vertol, Morton, Pennsylvania **Mission** Medium transport and assault helicopter **Service** US Marine Corps (CH-46A, CH-46D); US Navy (UH-46A, UH-46D)

CH/UH-46A SEA KNIGHT

Engine Two General Electric T58-GE-8B 1,250 shp shaft-turbine; **Rotor diameter** 50 ft (15.24 m); **Overall length** 83 ft 4 in (25.37 m); **Width** (blades folded) 14 ft 6¼ in (4.42 m); **Overall height** 16 ft 8½ in (5.09 m); **Weight** (empty) 12,406 lbs (5,627 kg), (loaded) 21,400 lbs (9,707 kg); **Maximum speed** (loaded, at sea level) 168 mph (270 km/h); **Cruising speed** (loaded) 155 mph (249 km/h); **Range** (loaded, with reserve) 230 miles (370 km); **Armament** None; **Accommodation** Crew of three, 26 troops.

CH/UH-46D SEA KNIGHT

Engine Two General Electric T58-GE-10 1,400 shp shaft-turbine; **Rotor diameter** 51 ft (15.54 m); **Overall length** 84 ft 3 in (25.67 m); **Width** (blades folded) 14 ft 6¼ in (4.42 m); **Overall height** 16 ft 8½ in (5.09 m); **Weight** (empty) 13,067 lbs (5,927 kg), (loaded) 23,000 lbs (10,432 kg); **Maximum speed** (loaded, at sea level) 166 mph (267 km/h); **Cruising speed** (loaded) 161 mph (259 km/h); **Range** (loaded) 238 miles (383 km); **Armament** None; **Accommodation** Crew of three, 26 troops.

Preliminary design on the Boeing-Vertol Model 107 (US Marine Corps and US Navy designation CH-46/UH-46 Sea Knight) commenced in 1956. The main objective was to take full advantage of the high power, small size and light weight of the shaft-turbine engines then becoming available. The best possible hovering performance was achieved by using the traditional Vertol tandem-rotor layout, and the turbines were mounted above the rear of the cabin permitting a large, unobstructed cabin space into which vehicles and bulky supplies could be loaded by means of a long rear ramp.

The US Army considered the CH-46 too heavy for the assault role and too light for the transport role, and it was this decision which led the Army to upgrade the more manoeuvrable Bell UH-1 Iroquois (Huey) as a tactical troop transport and to acquire a heavy transport helicopter in the form of the CH-47 Chinook, which came from the same Boeing-Vertol stable. Both the Marines and the Navy, however, wanted the Sea Knight, and alternative versions of the Model 107 were supplied to the Royal Canadian Air Force (CH-133 Labrador), the Canadian Army (CH-1113A Voyageur)

In the South China Sea, a Navy UH-46A Sea Knight helicopter prepares to lift an artillery piece from the deck of the Dock Landing Ship USS Monticello (LSD-35) for delivery to a beach in support of a 'search and destroy' mission against the North Vietnamese and Viet Cong just south of the DMZ in 1967.

and the Royal Swedish Air Force and Navy (HKP-4).

Used mostly for routine supply work, cargoes could be swiftly loaded by one man. To simplify landing on the decks of aircraft carriers, a powered blade-folding system enabled the rotor blades to be folded quickly by a pilot-operated control. In the rescue role, the Sea Knight could lift 20 troops or 15 stretcher cases with two medical orderlies.

The first CH-46A flew on 16 October 1962, and four Marine squadrons were operating the aircraft by June 1965. Three months later the Department of Defense ordered Boeing to increase production of the CH-46A/D by 100 per cent, then, in March 1966, Sea Knights went into action in Vietnam. During their first two and a half years on active service they exceeded 100,000 combat flight hours. Generally similar to the CH-46A, the CH-46D Sea Knight had, however, an uprated General Electric engine and carried a

A Marine Corps re-supply Sea Knight helicopter delivers equipment for a new campsite in the Khe Sanh area while on Operation 'Utah Mesa' during June 1969.

heavier payload. A total of 425 CH-46/UH-46s had been delivered by 2 May 1968, and by June 1969 the US Marine Corps had received its 500th Sea Knight.

The US Navy's UH-46A Sea Knight, which was superseded in September 1966 by the UH-46D, was ordered by the Navy for combat supply ships; they were utilized to transfer supplies, ammunition, missiles and aviation spares from these ships to combatant vessels under way at sea. Secondary tasks included transfer of personnel and search and rescue. UH-46As had been deployed with the US Seventh Fleet in the South China Sea from mid-1965, but the Vietnam War led to innovations in ship re-supply, including bad weather vertical replenishment (VERTREP) and night VERTREP with the aid of small signal lights.

The Sea Knights, probably because of their more mundane duties, did not share in the limelight enjoyed by its fellow twin-engined, twin-rotored helicopter, the US Army CH-47 Chinook. Marine Sea Knights were nevertheless greatly praised

A CH-46D Sea Knight helicopter of Marine Helicopter Squadron 165 (HMM-165) stands on the deck of the Amphibious Assault Ship USS New Orleans (LPH-11) during Operation 'End Sweep' in February 1973.

for running in supplies in the monsoon rains to Marines manning hilltop outposts during the battle that raged at Khe Sanh from late January to mid-April 1968. Like the Marine H-34s employed on the Khe Sanh sorties, the Sea Knights were unarmed and had to rely on the HueyCobras to protect them.

Sea Knights of Marine Heavy Lift Helicopter Squadron (HMH) 463 were included in the helicopter force of the 31st Marine Amphibious Unit (Task Group 79.4) assembled on board the amphibious ship *Okinawa* and carrier *Hancock* in March 1975 to rescue American embassy officials and allied personnel from Phnom Penh, the capital of Cambodia. As the Khmer Rouge ring tightened around Phnom Penh, the resistance of the Cambodian government forces began to crumble, and it was anticipated that at least 800 people were in urgent need of rescue from the city.

On 7 April, the amphibious task force, which also included the amphibious ships *Vancouver*, *Thomaston* and surface escorts *Edson*, *Henry B. Wilson*, *Knox* and *Kir*, was placed on a three-hour alert and positioned off the Cambodian coast. Then, in the early hours of 12 April, the order to carry out the daring mission was received. At 0745 hours local time, *Okinawa* followed by *Hancock* began to launch helicopters in three waves carrying 350 men of the 2nd Battalion, 4th Marines, who would act as the ground security force defending the landing zones. One hour later, after traversing 100 miles (160 km), the HMH 462 helicopters from *Okinawa* and HMH 463 from *Hancock* set down near the US embassy at Phnom Penh and the Marines quickly established a defensive perimeter. Within the next two hours, US officials assembled the evacuees and expeditiously loaded them on the helicopters. As some of the people had already escaped by other means, the evacuees only numbered 276 — 82 US, 159 Cambodian and 35 other nationals.

By 1041 hours, all the evacuees had been lifted out, and little more than 30 minutes later the ground security force was also airborne and heading out to sea; at 1224 hours the aircraft and personnel were safely on board the ships of the amphibious task force. Although one Khmer Rouge 75 mm shell had landed near the embassy landing zone, no casualties were suffered during the entire operation. The following day, the task force helicopters flew the evacuees to Thailand and the naval force set sail for Subic Bay, its base in the Philippine Islands.

BOEING-VERTOL CH-47 CHINOOK

(A, B AND C MODELS)

Origin Boeing-Vertol, Morton, Pennsylvania **Mission** Transportation of cargo, equipment and troops **Service** US Army

Engine Two 2,200 shp Lycoming T55-L-5 or 2,650 shp T55-L-7 shaft-turbine (CH-47A), two 2,850 shp Lycoming T55-L-7C shaft-turbine (CH-47B), two 3,750 shp Lycoming T55-L-11 shaft-turbine (CH-47C); **Rotor diameter** 59 ft 1 in (17.9 m) (CH-47A), 60 ft 0 in (18.2 m) (CH-47B/C); **Overall length** 98 ft 1 in (29.8 m) (CH-47A), 99 ft 0 in (30.1 m) (CH-47B/C); **Width** (blades folded) 12 ft 5 in (3.72 m) (all models); **Overall height** 18 ft 7 in (5.65 m) (all models); **Weight** (empty) 18,112 lbs (8,215 kg) (CH-47A), 19,555 lbs (8,870 kg) (CH-47B), 20,547 lbs (9,320 kg) (CH-47C), (loaded) 31,512 lbs (18,293 kg) (CH-47A), 38,115 lbs (17,288 kg) (CH-47B), 43,997 lbs (19,957 kg) (CH-47C); **Maximum speed** (loaded, at sea level) 150 mph (241 km/h) (CH-47A); **Cruising speed** (loaded) 130 mph (209 km/h) (CH-47A); **Range** (loaded, with reserves) 250 miles (402 km) (CH-47A); **Armament** 7.62 mm door mounted machine-guns; **Accommodation** Two pilots on flight deck with dual controls, jump seat provided for crew chief or combat commander. Depending on seating arrangement, 33 to 44 troops in main cabin, or 24 stretchers plus two medical orderlies, or vehicles and freight. Typical loads included a complete artillery section with crew and ammunition, and missile systems such as Little John. All components of the Pershing missile system were transportable by Chinook.

A Boeing-Vertol CH-47 Chinook takes off from USS Boxer *shortly after its arrival in South Vietnamese waters on 12 September 1965.*

Chinooks from Marine Medium Helicopter Squadron 161, Marble Mountain Air Facility, transport Marines of the 1st Division to 'Arizona Territory' during an operation south of Danang in 1966.

The development of the CH-47 (formerly YHC-1A) Chinook series of helicopters began in 1956, when the Department of the Army announced its intention to replace its piston-engined H-37 transport helicopters with a new generation of turbine-powered machines. There were those in the US Army in the mid 1950s who felt that the new helicopter should be a light tactical transport aimed at the mission of the old H-21s and H-34s and, consequently, sized for approximately 15 troops. Another point of view, however, was that the new transport should be larger, to serve as an artillery transporter and be able to carry a Pershing missile system.

The first Vertol prototype, the YHC-1A, was built with a maximum troop capacity of twenty. This model, which eventually became Vertol's commercial 107 and the Marine Sea Knight, was considered by most of the Army to be too heavy for the assault role and too light for the transport role, so it finally settled on a larger Chinook as its medium transport helicopter, and the first hovering flight was made on 28 April 1961. By February 1966, 161 aircraft had been delivered to the Army, and the effectiveness of the CH-47 has been increased by successive product improvement programmes. A total of 550 Chinooks had been delivered by February 1969, at which time US Army CH-47s had flown more than 500,000 hours; of this total, more than two-thirds had been accumulated under combat conditions in South-east Asia.

The CH-47 was designed to meet the US Army's requirement for an all-weather medium transport helicopter and, depending on the series model, was capable of lifting specified payloads in severe combinations of altitude and temperature conditions; the primary mission radius was 115 miles (185 km). Boeing-Vertol announced in April 1969 that a Chinook had flown with composite material rotor blades; 60 ft (18.2 m) in diameter and constructed of glass-fibre with an aluminium honeycomb core, they were the largest composite material blades then made.

During the period of the Vietnam War, three versions of the CH-47 Chinook were in service. The CH-47As, the initial production model, were consigned with their Huey escorts to serve the 1st Cavalry Division to Vietnam in 1965. Twin-engined, with two sets of rotors, one above the cockpit and one at the rear, the CH-47A was fitted with two Lycoming gas turbines. The CH-47B, which first came off the assembly line on 10 May 1967, had uprated gas turbine engines, redesigned rotor blades with a cambered leading edge, and other minor modifications, to improve the aircraft's flying qualities.

The CH-47C, with its two 3,750 shp T55-L-11 gas turbine engines and increased integral fuel capacity, was by far the most powerful of the Chinooks. The first flight of a CH-47C was made on 14 October 1967, and deliveries of the production aircraft began in the spring of 1968; they were first deployed to Vietnam in September of that year. By the beginning of 1969, some 270 CH-47Cs were in action there, and had logged more than 300,000 hours of combat flight. On one occasion, no fewer than 147 refugees and their possessions were evacuated by a single aircraft, and also by that time Chinooks had picked up 5,700 disabled aircraft and flown them to repair bases.

If the Huey was the cavalry horse and endowed with the tradition of the US Cavalry of 'Old Army' years, the Chinook was more akin to Hannibal's elephants. The Huey became the cornerstone of air mobility, and the Chinook one of the principal building blocks.

The Chinooks assigned to the 1st Cavalry Division comprised a battalion, and a company, the 147th, was linked to the 1st US Infantry Division. The most spectacular mission in Vietnam for the Chinook was the placing of artillery batteries in mountain positions that were inaccessible by any other means, and then keeping them supplied with large quantities of ammunition.

The infantryman worldwide has for centuries depended on artillery for support whether on the offensive or in retreat. The

Paratroopers of the 2nd Bn, 327th Infantry, 1st Brigade, 101st Airborne Division await airlift by a CH-47 to take them to Bao Loc in 1968.

artilleryman in turn has depended on the infantry to secure his positions and keep his supply routes open. In Vietnam no simple solutions were available to continue this long-established team-work. Originally hauled by teams of horses, it was not until the Second World War that field guns achieved any real mobility with the use of wheeled and tracked vehicles powered by the internal combustion engine. Even so, whereas the tank-like self-propelled guns, which are an item of artillery, could move more or less at will, much sweat was needed, especially in muddy conditions, to manhandle the guns into and out of their firing lines.

The nature of the guerrilla war in Vietnam with its jungled highlands, lowlands and labyrinthine delta waterways meant that there were no front lines from which the allies — or the enemy — could advance from or fall back to. As for the infantry, the helicopter provided the means of mounting short-term 'search and destroy missions' with adequate fire support. The early designers of the airmobile division had recognized that they would have to sacrifice the heavy 155 mm howitzers and be content with moving the 105 mm howitzer with the Chinook helicopter.

The 1st Cavalry Division found that its Chinooks were limited to a 7,000 lbs (3,175 kg) payload when operating in the mountains, but could carry an additional 1,000 lbs when operating near the coast. The early Chinook design was limited by its rotor system which did not permit full use of the installed power, and the users were anxious for an improved version which would upgrade this system.

As it turned out, a 155 mm howitzer battalion was continuously attached to the 1st Cavalry Division. It was teamed with the CH-54 Tarhe Sky Crane to become an integral part of the Air Cavalry's fire support. The Little John rocket had been included in the original line-up, but when the 1st Cavalry deployed to Vietnam, the Little John was left out due to tactical and manpower considerations. The aerial artillery battalion was organized as the general support artillery, and the personnel serving three firing batteries were lifted in twelve Huey helicopters armed with 2.75 in aerial rockets.

During a major assault the air was filled with hundreds of troop transport helicopters, armed helicopters, reconnaissance aircraft and tactical air support. Through this dense formation thousands of shells from tube artillery had to travel, so fire support co-ordination during the critical air assault phase was difficult to achieve with perfection. The tactical air support, tube and aerial artillery, sometimes naval gunfire and B-52 bomber schedules, all had to be integrated without danger to the friendly forces and without firepower gaps that would relieve pressure on the enemy.

During the first battle of the Ia Drang Valley, the 1st Cavalry

Right A Chinook helicopter lifts a disabled Huey troop-carrier from LZ 'X-Ray' in the Ia Drang Valley where it was shot down by North Vietnamese gunners of the 320th NVA Regiment in 1966.

Below left Chinooks re-supply US Marines during the heavy fighting for Khe Sanh in March 1968. The Marines manned outposts in the hills surrounding the fire base.

Below A Chinook airlifts a 105-mm howitzer to the Suoi Da area near Tay Ninh City during Operation 'Attleboro' in November 1966.

A cavalryman hooks a sling attached to a CH-47 Chinook to an M-113 Armoured Personnel Carrier which has become bogged down in a paddy field near Cu Chi in October 1968.

covered such a wide zone that the siting of artillery was of the utmost importance. Not only was it necessary for the prior arrivals to cover the landing zones of the incoming assault forces, but it was also necessary to place the guns in such a position that they could cover other artillery in co-ordinated fire plans. In previous conflicts, when conducting indirect fire the gunners, apart from the forward observers, would not actually have seen the enemy positions. In Vietnam, with the Viet Cong maybe lurking in the nearby trees and bushes, the artilleryman frequently found himself face to face with the enemy and deserved to be recognized, in addition to his assigned role, as a true combat infantryman.

The challenge to the CH-47s and CH-54s will be appreciated if the clear distinction between aerial artillery and the roving gunship is understood. The gunship was available at base or already roving the sky prepared for instant reaction to calls for fire support. The helicopter-borne guns, on the other hand, were flown in section by section, landing wave after wave in a location only a matter of a few minutes away from the target area. Continuous fire support was

A Chinook helicopter brings in a load of 105-mm howitzer rounds for an ARVN battery at Fire Base 'Maureen', situated 16 miles west-south-west of Hue, in August 1970.

thus ensured for the infantry until such times as guns and crews were picked up and flown into another landing zone in the battle area.

With the success of the Chinook as a prime artillery mover and heavy cargo carrier, its intended role as a medium assault helicopter was quietly forgotten. However, an armed version of the CH-47, unique to the 1st Cavalry Division, was the so-called 'Go-Go Bird'. The 'Go-Go Bird', as named by the Infantry, was a heavily armed Chinook which the 1st Cavalry was asked to test in combat. Three test models were armed with twin 20 mm Gatling guns, 40 mm grenade launchers and .50 calibre machine-guns, along with assorted ordnance. Though anything but graceful, they had a tremendous morale effect on the friendly troops who constantly asked for their support.

From the GI's viewpoint, when the 'Go-Go Bird' came the enemy disappeared, and the pilots who flew these test machines performed some incredibly heroic deeds to prove its worth. However, the armed Chinook required an inordinate amount of

A CH-47 of the 'Air Cav' takes off with a 105-mm howitzer from Fire Base 'Custer', which is being pulled back to Bien Hoa in March 1971.

maintenance support and the 1st Cavalry found they could keep three Chinook lift ships in the air for the price of one 'Go-Go Bird'. When two of the armed Hueys became unairworthy through attrition, the final 'Go-Go Bird' was transferred to the 1st Aviation Brigade. Although judged a mistake, the troopers, who had enjoyed its support, never forgot it.

The CH-47 was also deployed as a 'bomber' over South Vietnam. The Viet Cong developed an ingenious and wide-ranging underground fortification and tunnel system throughout Binh Dinh Province. Many of these fortifications could withstand almost any explosion, so tear gas was introduced to drive the enemy into the open. During Operation 'Pershing' in 1967, the 1st Cavalry dropped a total of 29,000 lbs (12,247 kg) of tear gas from CH-47 helicopters using a simple, locally fabricated fusing system on a standard drum.

Initially the drums were merely rolled out of the back of the open door and the fusing system was armed by a static line after it was free of the aircraft. Using this method, a large concentration of tear gas could be spread over a suspected area with accuracy. Napalm was rigged and dropped in a similar manner during this same period; a single CH-47 could drop 2½ tons of napalm on an enemy installation. Naturally, this was only used on specific targets where tactical air support could not be effectively used.

HUGHES OH-6A CAYUSE

Origin Hughes Tool Company, Aircraft Division, Culver City, California
Mission Visual observation and target acquisition, reconnaissance, command and control **Service** US Army

Engine One Allison T63-A-5A 317 shp shaft-turbine; **Rotor diameter** 26 ft 4 in (8.02 m); **Overall length** 30 ft 3¾ in (9.23 m); **Skid track** 6 ft 9 in (2.05 m); **Overall height** (to top of rotor hub) 8 ft 1½ in (2.47 m); **Weight** (empty) 1,229 lbs (557 kg), (loaded) 2,400 lbs (1,088 kg); **Maximum speed** (loaded, at sea level) 150 mph (241 km/h); **Cruising speed** (loaded) 134 mph (215 km/h); **Range** 380 miles (611 km); **Armament** Provision for packaged armament on port side of fuselage comprising XM-27 7.62 mm machine-gun (2,000-4,000 rounds per minute) or XM-75 grenade launcher; **Accommodation** Crew of two seated side-by-side in front, two seats in rear cargo compartment or, seats folded, four fully-equipped soldiers seated on the floor.

The Hughes OH-6A (formerly HO-6) Cayuse was chosen for development following a US Army design competition for a light observation helicopter in 1961. The US Defense Department were in fact envisaging a single helicopter to perform such duties as personnel or cargo transport, light ground attack, casualty evacuation, observation, and photographic reconnaissance. The OH-6A was the result, but in South Vietnam the Cayuse proved most effective at nap-of-the-earth reconnaissance, searching for

The first two OH-6A Cayuse light observation helicopters to arrive in South Vietnam await installation of the rotor blades at Tan Son Nhut Air Base in March 1967.

In May 1968, a Cayuse of the 7th Squadron (Airmobile), 17th Cavalry, leads troops to a spot near Pleiku where the pilot has spotted a suspected enemy bunker complex.

signs of the Viet Cong. Skimming over the tree tops, its crew kept their eyes peeled for tell-tale smoke from a fire that might mark a VC hide, tracks suggesting recent movement, or other signs of enemy activity.

In 1970, the OH-6A joined with the AH-1G HueyCobra gunship as 'Pink Teams' to screen the deployment of air cavalry troops, and they proved their worth as requirements mounted for support of more and more operations over larger and larger areas. The Cayuse/Cobra combination was most effective in the Cambodian Campaign; on the final day of the operation, 29 June 1970, every possible precaution was taken in the actual crossing of the border by US troops to ensure success. Troop ladders, smoke ships, pathfinders and recovery aircraft were available to cover any contingency. In the event, the crossing proved uneventful, with the last CH-47 Chinook aircraft leaving Cambodia at 1523 hours. The honour of being the last US Army aircraft out of Cambodia went to B Company of the 1st Squadron, 9th Cavalry (the elite 'Cav of the Cav'), whose screening 'Pink Team' reported re-entering Vietnam at 1728 hours, 29 June. The 'Cav of the Cav' had proved conclusively in the Cambodian Campaign how invaluable the 'Pink

Top *A crew chief loads a mini-gun on an OH-6A Cayuse at a location near Mai Loc.*

Above *OH-6As from the 101st Airborne Division sit in line on a helicopter pad without any protective revetments in the Khe Sanh area in February 1971.*

Team' capability was to an airmobile operation.

During the whole of May and June 1970, the Squadron performed intensive ground and aerial reconnaissance operations almost every flyable hour. The Squadron's assets were shifted as necessary, capitalizing on mobility, reconnaissance and firepower

Above *A UH-34G Seahorse helicopter of Helicopter Training Squadron Eight (HT-8) lifts a heavy block in 1967.*

Below *A SEAL/UDT Navy commando is picked up by a CH-46 Sea Knight during a demonstration in the Pacific.*

Above *ARVN airborne troops unload from CH-47 Chinook helicopters at Landing Zone 'Stud', Khe Sanh, in April 1968.*

Below *A UH-1D from the 9th Helicopter Squadron, Royal Australian Air Force, takes off for Nui Dat in July 1970 after bringing in supplies to members of the 2nd ANZAC Bn.*

Above *A CH-54 'Flying Crane' airlifts a 105-mm towed howitzer into Fire Base 'Abby' in 1970, operated by the 1st Bn, 14th Artillery, 23rd Infantry Division.*

Below *An AH-1G Cobra gunship from Troop 'D', 3rd Squadron, 4th Cavalry, returns to Cu Chi from operations in Cambodia in 1970.*

Above *A Sikorsky HH-3E 'Jolly Green Giant' of 46th Aerospace Rescue & Recovery Squadron flies from Eglin Air Force Base, Florida, during 1967.*

Below *A US Air Force HH-53 'Super Jolly Green Giant' seen in flight near Udorn Royal Thai Air Force Base in 1968.*

in order to determine enemy locations and escape routes. The Cobra/Cayuse teams enabled the Air Cavalry troops to cover large areas effectively, and, when the situation warranted, the aero-rifle platoon would be inserted to face the enemy until a larger force could be committed to the area. The intelligence provided by the 1st Squadron, 9th Cavalry, assisted the 1st Cavalry Division in the redeployment of its assets and the destruction of many of the enemy's large cache sites.

In August 1970, General Putnam directed an analysis of the productivity of the aircraft assets of the 1st Cavalry Division. This analysis disclosed that airlift escort by a section of two Cobras from the gun company of the airlift battalions was the least productive mission being flown by the division. It was determined therefore that the escort at that time could be abandoned since aerial rocket artillery (fixed-wing) gunships were always posted at the critical points, the pick-up and landing zones.

The analysis also revealed that essential general support missions normally flown by OH-6As could be supported by fewer aircraft if careful controls were maintained. Based on these findings, two provisional air cavalry troops were formed using the Assault Weapons Companies of the 227th and 229th Assault Helicopter Battalions and attaching necessary OH-6s and personnel from other Divisional units. This enlarged the air cavalry squadron to five troops and greatly increased the Division's capability to cover its far-flung operations.

KAMAN HH-43 HUSKIE

Origin Kaman Aerospace Corporation (a subsidiary of Kaman Corporation), Hartford, Bloomfield, Windsor Locks and Moosup, Connecticut
Mission Crash rescue helicopter **Service** US Air Force, Aerospace Rescue and Recovery Service

HH-43B

Engine One Lycoming T53-L-1B 1,860 shp (derated to 1,825 shp) shaft-turbine; **Rotor diameter** (each) 47 ft (14.32 m); **Overall length** 25 ft 2 in (7.68 m); **Wheel track** 8 ft 4 in (2.53 m); **Overall height** 15 ft 6½ in (4.73 m); **Weight** (empty) 4,469 lbs (2,027 kg), (loaded) 5,969 lbs (2,707 kg); **Maximum speed** (loaded, at sea level) 120 mph (192 km/h); **Cruising speed** (loaded) 110 mph (177 km/h); **Range** (loaded) 277 miles (445 km).

HH-43F

Engine One Lycoming T53-L-11A 1,150 eshp (derated to 825 shp) shaft-turbine; **Rotor diameter, Overall length, Wheel track, Overall height** as HH-43B; **Weight** (empty) 4,620 lbs (2,095 kg), (loaded) 6,500 lbs (2,948 kg); **Maximum speed, Cruising speed** as HH-43B; **Range** 504 miles (811 km); **Armament** None; **Accommodation** Two crew and six passengers.

The Kaman Model 600-3/5 (USAF designation HH-43 Huskie) was a turbine-powered development of the piston-engined OH-/UH-/HH-43 series of helicopters. It flew for the first time on 27 September 1956, and there were two production versions, the

A UH-43 Huskie helicopter delivers passengers and mail to the US Navy's destroyer escort USS Conway *(DDE-507) in 1960. The Huskie was seen more familiarly in the US Air Force Air Rescue role from the early days in the Vietnam War.*

HH-43B and HH-43F, the former first flying in December 1958 and the latter in August 1964. They served in South-east Asia from the earliest days of the American involvement.

An important feature of the HH-43B/F, which incorporated Kaman's contra-rotating and intermeshing twin-rotor systems with servo-flap control, was that these versions had twice the cabin space and payload capacity of the piston-engined HH-43A, the increased space having been gained by mounting the lighter and more compact turbine engine above the cabin and between the rotor pylons instead of to the rear of the cabin. Repositioning of the engine had also made possible the installation of large clam-shell doors, forming the rear of the cabin. The raised tail unit was controlled by an auto-stabilizer.

Original orders for a total of 116 HH-43B Huskies were supplemented by further contracts for both this version and the HH-43F. The helicopters were primarily used, and with outstanding success, as local crash rescue helicopters at USAF bases throughout the world, while several foreign governments bought them for internal security, VIP transport and communications duties. The variety of loads included a pilot, two fully-clothed fire-fighters and 1,000 lbs (453 kg) of fire-fighting and rescue gear; pilot, co-pilot and six passengers; or pilot, medical orderly and four stretcher cases.

In the early 1960s, the HH-43, which was classified as a short-range helicopter, was the only crash rescue helicopter in the US Air Force inventory. The concept of the role and limited financial support of the late 1950s had forced the Air Rescue Service to give up most of its helicopters, but the usefulness of the Huskie was proven for fire-fighting and picking up pilots who had bailed out in close proximity to the airbase. In 1963, a batch of Sikorsky CH-3s were allocated to the air rescue role in Vietnam, but were diverted to the space recovery and astronaut recovery mission.

As an alternative, the Air Rescue Service decided to modify the HH-43B to make it better suited for combat aircrew recovery. Modifications included the addition of armour plate, the installation of a larger self-sealing fuel tank, a larger engine, and gun mounts, and the modified version was redesignated the HH-43F. However, the Kaman Aircraft Corporation indicated that these improvements would not be completed until October 1964, so in March it was six HH-4Bs, three from Pacific Air Command (PACAF) and three from Air Force units in the United States, that arrived in South Vietnam.

In June 1964 two HH-43 companies, including 36 personnel on temporary duty, were deployed to Nakhon Phanom, Thailand, thus bringing the Huskies within range of northern Laos. On 9 September 1964, the chief of staff of the Air Force, General Curtis

LeMay, approved the despatch of six HH-43Fs to Vietnam with heavy armour plating and 250 ft (76.2 m) long cables to facilitate rescues in the high rain forest; they arrived at Bien Hoa on 20 October. By November 1964, the Air Rescue commitment in South-east Asia included six bases in South Vietnam and Thailand.

More HH-43B/F rescue helicopters were on their way to Vietnam by the end of 1964 but there was a disadvantage in that the Huskies could not reach parts of Laos and North Vietnam from their bases in South Vietnam. The combat-modified F model, with its 350 gallon self-sealing fuel tank, had a greatly improved range over the B model and its 800 lbs (362 kg) of titanium armour distributed in half-inch (1.27 cm) sheet around the crew compartment also gave it better protection. It also scored over the B in its uprated Lycoming engine and its combination of very high frequency and frequency modulation sets which provided the helicopter crews with improved communications aids to co-ordinate rescue activities.

The HH-34F was further fitted with a jungle penetrator, making it better able to reach survivors through jungle canopy. This device incorporated spring-loaded arms that parted the jungle foliage as it was lowered to the survivor who, after strapping himself to the penetrator, released a set of spring-loaded arms at the other end to protect himself as he was hauled up through the branches of the trees. The jungle penetrator was used throughout the war and was responsible for lifting numerous survivors from the South-east Asian rain forests.

A typical search and rescue operation for the period occurred on 23 June 1965, when Major Robert Wilson's F-105 was hit by ground fire while on a mission over south-western North Vietnam. He was unable to fly his damaged Thunderchief over a ridgeline, so he ejected and after a normal descent he found himself suspended upside down in a tree 150 ft (46 m) above the jungle floor. He managed to swing into a fork of the tree where he freed himself from his parachute harness. He then took out his survival knife and cut a small branch from the tree which he used to snag his seatpack containing all his survival equipment.

Retrieving his URC-11 survival radio, Wilson contacted the HC-54 airborne command rescue post called 'Crown' which, in response to his Mayday, moved off its orbit along the Thai-Laotian border and soon afterwards flew by. Half-an-hour later, four Air Force A-1 Skyraiders droned into view, contacted the survivor and soon spotted Wilson's 'chute. After radioing the downed pilot's exact position to 'Crown', they then flew to an orbit several miles away so as not to reveal Wilson's location to any enemy troops that might be in the vicinity.

Ninety minutes after Wilson's ejection, an HH-43 from a forward operating base in Laos arrived. Wilson fired off a small flare that was part of his survival equipment, the Huskie pilot spotted it and moved his chopper directly overhead while the parajumper lowered the penetrator through the foliage. Wilson grabbed it, strapped himself on, and began his ascent to the helicopter. A few hours later Major Wilson arrived safely at Nakhon Phanom.

The summer of 1965 was a watershed period for search and rescue in South-east Asia. Trained air rescue crews, flying HHL-43Fs and CH-3Cs, provided a viable aircrew recovery capability. In addition to the arrival of the Jolly Green Giants, HC-54s replaced HU-16 amphibians in the airborne mission control role. At the end of the war the Air Rescue Service inventory in the area included six HH-3Es; one CH-3C (on loan from Tactical Air Command); 25 HH-43B/Fs; five HU-16s; and two HC-54s. All aircraft and personnel were assigned or attached to the 38th Air Rescue Squadron. The expanding rescue mission was beginning to receive the aircraft it needed.

By January 1966, the Air Force had activated the 3rd Aerospace Rescue and Recovery Group at Tan Son Nhut to serve as the primary rescue agency in South-east Asia. Besides the HH-43s at Nakhon Phanom and Bien Hoa, the Air Force employed HU-16 seaplanes to rescue pilots downed at sea. Ten rescue detachments were based throughout South Vietnam and four in Thailand, and in order to extend their operations rescue crews sought clearings in the jungle or remote mountain tops where they could stockpile fuel to await calls for help.

When President Richard Nixon commenced the 'Vietnamization' programme in 1969, involving the gradual withdrawal of American forces, rescue operations still continued until the ceasefire in 1973. By this time most of the HH-53s had been withdrawn from South-east Asia and were assigned to rescue units throughout the world. Some of the HH-43s reached local base rescue units in the United States, while others became part of a military assistance package for the Royal Thai Air Force.

Further sweeping changes occurred when, on 1 July 1971, the entire 38th Aerospace Rescue and Recovery Squadron, the unit that managed the HH-43s in South-east Asia, was deactivated. Planning for the ceasefire resulted in the almost total withdrawal of rescue forces from Vietnam by December 1972. On 30 November, the 37th Aerospace and Recovery Squadron at Danang was activated and five of its HH-53s were transferred to Nakhon Phanom Royal Thai Air Force Base, while just two HH-43s remained at Danang in the closing months of the American involvement in the Vietnam War.

KAMAN UH-2 SEASPRITE

Origin Kaman Aerospace Corporation (a subsidiary of Kaman Corporation), Hartford, Bloomfield, Windsor Locks and Moosup, Connecticut **Mission** General purpose helicopter **Service** US Navy

Engine One General Electric T58-GE-8B 1,250 shp shaft-turbine (UH-2A/B), two T58-GE-8F 1,350 shp shaft-turbine (UH-2C); **Rotor diameter** 44 ft (13.41 m); **Overall length** (blades turning) 52 ft 7 in (16.02 m); **Wheel track** (outer wheels) 10 ft 10 in (3.30 m); **Overall height** (blades turning) 15 ft 6 in (4.72 m); **Weight** (empty) 6,216 lbs (2,819 kg) (UH-2A), 6,099 lbs (2,766 kg) (UH-2B), 7,390 lbs (3,352 kg) (UH-2C), (loaded) 8,637 lbs (3,917 kg) (UH-2A/B), 9,951 lbs (4,513 kg) (UH-2C); **Maximum speed** (loaded, at sea level) 162 mph (260.7 km/h) (UH-2A/B), 157 mph (252 km/h) (UH-2C); **Cruising speed** (loaded) 150 mph (241 km/h) (all models); **Range** (loaded) 670 miles (1,078 km) (UH-2A/B), 425 miles (683 km) (UH-2C); **Armament** TAT-102A turret system with 7.62 mm minigun; **Accommodation** Two crew and up to 11 passengers or four stretcher patients. Could pick up 12 survivors in emergency sea rescue operations.

A Kaman UH-2 Seasprite of the US Navy, based on the attack aircraft carrier USS Forrestal *(CVA-19), seen in action in the Gulf of Tonkin, North Vietnam, in July 1967.*

A UH-2C Seasprite helicopter sets down on the flight deck of the nuclear-powered attack aircraft carrier USS Enterprise *(CVAN-65) in the Sea of Japan, April 1969.*

The Seasprite was capable of performing a variety of missions, including all-weather search and rescue, plane guard, casualty evacuation, gunfire observation, courier service, reconnaissance, personnel transfer, radiological reconnaissance, vertical replenishment, tactical air control, wire-laying, emergency supply and resupply, towing and operation from small ships. It was equipped with the latest electronic equipment for all-weather navigation, automatic stabilization, auto-navigation, water flotation and in-flight blade tracking, while an external cargo hook with a 4,000 lb (1,814 kg) capacity was standard equipment.

The first UH-2A deliveries were made to the US Navy's squadron HU-2 in December 1962 and first shipped to sea aboard USS *Independence* in June 1963. Two months later the UH-2B was assigned to USS *Albany*, and both types were used extensively in South-east Asia. In March 1965, Kaman aircraft completed a conversion programme to instal two T58-GE-8 engines in pods on either side of the rotor pylon to improve the Seasprite's performance. Starting in 1967, UH-2As and UH-2Bs were converted to become UH-2Cs; about one hundred such conversions were completed by the spring of 1968.

The US Army acquired a small batch of UH-2s and named the aircraft Tomahawk. One aircraft was fitted with a 1,500 shp T58-GE-10 engine and evaluated in the ground support role, with an M-60 four-gun turret in the nose and launching pylons on the cabin sides for minigun pods, 40 mm grenade launchers, pods of unguided rockets, or anti-tank missiles. One HH-2D, announced late in 1969, was identical to the HH-2C, except that the armament and armour were deleted.

The SH-2D was the interim Light Airborne Multi-Purpose System (LAMPS) version of the HH-2D, for ASW and missile defence. The modification involved the installation of a high-power search radar in a chin mount, sonobuoys, magnetic anomaly detector, associated electronic monitors and controls, smoke markers and flares. Hard mounts for MK-46 homing torpedoes were also included. The first deliveries of the HH-2Ds were made in the summer of 1971, the SH-2D version making its inaugural flight at Bloomfield, Connecticut, on 31 March of that year. The SH-2Ds commenced operational deployment in November 1971, some operating from guided missile frigates.

SIKORSKY CH-54 TARHE

Origin Sikorsky Aircraft, Division of the United Aircraft Corporation, Stratford, Connecticut **Mission** Movement of heavy outsized loads, recovery of downed aircraft, and, by use of detachable pods, transportation of personnel, vehicles and equipment **Service** US Army

Engine Two 4,050 shp Pratt & Whitney JFTD12A-1 shaft-turbine; **Rotor diameter** 72 ft (21.9 m); **Overall length** 88 ft 6 in (26.9m); **Width** (blades folded) 21 ft 10 in (6.6 m); **Overall height** 18 ft 7 in (5.6 m); **Weight** (empty) 18,217 lbs (8,263 kg), (loaded) 42,000 lbs (19,051 kg); **Maximum speed** (loaded, at sea level) 127 mph (204 km/h); **Cruising speed** (loaded) 109 mph (175 km/h); **Range** (loaded, no reserve) 278 miles (447 km); **Armament** None; **Accommodation** Three crew, pilot and co-pilot sitting side-by-side at front of cabin. Aft-facing seat with flying controls for third pilot at rear of cabin, who was able to take over control of the aircraft during loading and unloading. Two additional jump seats available in cabin. Payload in interchangeable pods (see below).

The Sikorsky S-64A Sky Crane twin-turbine helicopter, US military designation CH-54A, was designed for universal military transport duties. Equipped with interchangeable pods (similar to freight containers), the CH-54A was suitable for use as a 67-seat troop transport, mine-sweeper and cargo and missile transporter and in anti-submarine or field hospital operations. Equipment included a 15,000 lb (6,804 kg) hoist, a sling attachment and a load stabilizer to prevent undue sway in cargo winch operations. Attachment

A Sikorsky CH-54A Tarhe ('Flying Crane') lowers a damaged CV-2 Caribou transport plane on to the ground at Qui Nhon. The 'Flying Crane' has just lifted the 14,000 lb (6,350 kg) aircraft 50 miles from where it crashed at Tuy Hoa in March 1966.

A 'Flying Crane' of the 222nd Combat Support Aviation Battalion prepares to pick up a truck from the deck of HMAS Sydney, an Australian aircraft carrier anchored in Vung Tau Harbour in 1968.

points were provided on the fuselage and landing gear to facilitate securing of bulky loads, and the pick-up of loads was made easier by the pilot's ability to shorten or extend the landing gear hydraulically.

The first of three prototypes of the S-64A flew for the first time on 9 May 1962, and was used by the US Army at Fort Benning, Georgia, for testing and demonstration, while the second and third prototypes were delivered to Federal Germany for evaluation by the German armed forces. In June 1963, the US Army announced that it had ordered six S-64As, under the designation CH-54A (originally YCH-54A), to investigate the heavy lift concept, with emphasis on increasing mobility on the battlefield; five were delivered in late 1964 and early 1965.

The CH-54As were assigned to the US Army's 478th Aviation Company, which went into action with the 1st Cavalry Division in Vietnam in September 1965. In April, before leaving the United States, the commanding officer of the 478th, Major T. J. Clark, and Chief Warrant Officer U. V. Brown set up three new international height records in a Sky Crane. They reached an altitude of 21,374 ft (6,506 m) with a 11,020 lb (5,000 kg) payload; 28,743 ft (8,749 m) with 4,410 lbs (2,000 kg); and 29,340 ft (9,053 m) with 2,204 lbs (1,000 kg). Later in the same month, a CH-54A of the 478th

Company lifted 90 persons, including 87 combat-equipped troops, in a 'people's pod' detachable van. This was believed at the time to be the largest number of persons ever carried by a helicopter in one lift.

In Vietnam, the Tarhe, which had a greater lift capacity than the Chinook, transported heavy artillery ordnance such as the 155 mm howitzer, positioning the guns often in difficult mountain terrain, and picked up downed aircraft. Sky Cranes could transport bulldozers and road graders weighing up to 17,500 lbs (7,938 kg) each, and armoured vehicles of 20,000 lbs (9,072 kg), as well as other heavy hardware. The CH-54s retrieved more than 380 damaged aircraft valued at $210 million.

The 1st Air Cavalry Division, specializing in the instant reaction airborne role, worked from the early autumn of 1965 with other kindred 'ever ready' units. Foremost amongst these was the 173rd Airborne Brigade, which, as the Army's combat spearhead, flew in from its strategic reserve base on Okinawa to the airfield at Vung Tau to protect the major air base at Bien Hoa. During the month of June, the 'Sky Soldiers' — as they were to be known — were joined by the 1st Battalion, the Royal Australian Regiment, and a field battery from New Zealand. On 28 June, this allied force combined with other units to conduct the largest troop lift operation in the Republic of South Vietnam up to that time. Over 144 Army aircraft, including 77 troop transport helicopters, also lifted two battalions of the Vietnamese 2nd Airborne Brigade and the 1st and 2nd Battalions deep into the area the French had called 'War Zone D'. After a successful strike, the 'Sky Soldiers' with the Australians and ARVN returned to the same area on 6 July to make multiple air assaults just north of the Song Dong Nai River. Some 1,494 helicopter sorties were flown on that occasion.

The other crack unit in the Vietnam War from the beginning was the 1st Brigade, the 101st 'Screaming Eagles' Airborne Division, whose battle honours in 1944-45 included Normandy, Holland, the Ardennes and the pursuit into Germany. The 1st Brigade was joined by the 2nd Brigade during the Tet Offensive in 1968, thus forming the second US airmobile division in Vietnam. The rappelling technique, mentioned elsewhere in connection with casualty retrieval by the 'Dust-Off' crews, was pioneered for the infantry by the 'Screaming Eagles'; ropes dangling from helicopters were used by the 'pathfinders' who slid down them into thick jungle to hack out landing zones.

A major 'search and destroy' mission was launched against the Viet Cong on 22 February 1967, which was to be the peak year for helicopters in the Vietnam War. Operation 'Junction City' employed the 173rd Airborne Brigade in an initial parachute assault, the 1st and 25th Infantry Divisions, the 11th Armoured

A CH-54 'Flying Crane' of the 1st Cavalry Division (Airmobile) hovers over 'Laramie', a mountain-top artillery position in the central highlands, in 1967.

Cavalry Regiment, the 196th Light Infantry Brigade and South Vietnamese units. Their target was enemy bases north of Tay Ninh City.

The requirement for helicopters on 'D-Day' was substantial. The 1st Infantry Division had five battalions to place by air assault and the 173rd had three battalions. In addition to the demand for the Huey 'slicks', there was a heavy requirement for CH-47s and Sky Cranes to lift and position artillery and resupply with ammunition. The 173rd had computed that they would free 60 Hueys and six Chinooks by parachuting in from Hercules C-130s. However, there was a stronger, emotional reason for the 'Sky Soldiers' wanting to jump; with helicopters taking over the airborne assault role, they felt they needed to justify their parachute brevets, and jump pay was hard to come by in the Vietnam War.

A battalion of the 173rd jumped on schedule, and by 0920 hours on 'D-Day' all companies were in their locations around the dropping zone (DZ). The heavy equipment drop commenced at 0925 hours and continued throughout the day. The 1st Battalion, 503rd Infantry, began landing in helicopters at 1035 hours and the entire battalion was in place shortly afterwards. Operation 'Junction City', which lasted three weeks, inflicted 2,700 losses on the Viet Cong, and vast amounts of ammunition, medical supplies and rice were captured. Army aviation lifted 9,518 troops and a daily average of 50 tons of cargo.

For its first 19 months in Vietnam, the 1st Cavalry Division had operated in I Corps Tactical Zone. However, on 7 April 1967 the 'Air Cav' went in pursuit of the Viet Cong in Quang Ngai Province, the southern boundary of which lay on the line of demarcation between I and II Corps. Tactical Zone I Corps was the responsibilty of the USMC and the enemy felt they would be safe from helicopters in the Quang Ngai area. Operation 'Lejeune', which was a combined 1st Cavalry and Marine Corps operation, lasted 15 days and was an unqualified success. The use of airmobile tactics took the enemy by surprise and the effectiveness of the operation was greatly enhanced by the construction of two airstrips in just a few days. The need for a heavy-duty airstrip was recognized immediately after the first assault, and the decision was made to quickly build a C-7A Caribou strip at landing zone 'Montezuma', which could be expanded to accommodate C-123 aircraft. At 'Montezuma' there would also be space enough to build a parallel Caribou strip while the first airstrip was improved and surfaced to handle the larger and heavier 'trash haulers' (C-130s).

A 13,000 lb (5,895 kg) armoured vehicle is manoeuvred on to its tracks as it is lowered by a 'Flying Crane' at a forward patrol base in 1970.

A sling has been attached to a CH-47 Chinook and the slack is taken up by the CH-54's winch while crewmen prepare to dismount from the Chinook. This particular mission of the 273rd Heavy Helicopter Company in February 1971 was to move this damaged Chinook from Bear Cat to Tan Son Nhut Air Base.

Company B of the 8th Engineer Battalion had arrived at LZ 'Montezuma' during the morning of the 7th and were now ordered to check out the proposed airfield. During the next two days, 31 pieces of heavy engineer equipment weighing over 200 tons were airlifted into Duc Pho, requiring 29 CH-54 'Flying Crane' and 15 Chinook sorties. Much of the equipment had to be partially dismantled to reduce the weight to a transportable helicopter load, but by 1800 hours on the 7th enough equipment was on the ground to begin work.

By 1630 on the afternoon of 8 April, the 1,500 ft (456.6 m) strip was completed, but work continued to expand it to 2,300 ft (700 m) for C-123 use. The first Caribous carried the mundane cargo of a culvert, which, since no parking ramp had yet been prepared, was unloaded by the side of the runway. On 13 April, the 8th Engineers began the construction of the second Caribou airstrip parallel and west of the completed C-123 strip, and this was finished in 25

A maintenance platoon at work on a CH-54 at their facility on Freedom Hill near Danang in July 1970.

hours after 4,150 cu yds (3,173 cu m) of earth had been moved and graded.

Probably no single operation better demonstrated the airmobile concept than the 1st Cavalry Division's Cambodian campaign. Beginning in the autumn of 1968, the 1st Cavalry had straddled the enemy trails leading southwards from the Cambodian border to Saigon. Having achieved some success in 1969 in blocking the Ho Chi Minh Trail, it was decided to send US and ARVN troops into Cambodia to hit concentrations of NVA troops and Viet Cong supplies. 'D-Day' was 1 May 1970, which marked the commencement of a 60-day campaign. Besides the 1st Cavalry's own Cranes, the 273rd Aviation Company (Heavy Helicopter) was under the operational control of the 1st Cavalry during the campaign. This company, with its CH-54s, lifted engineering equipment (272 bulldozers, 54 backhoes and 41 road graders) as well as the 155 mm howitzers into (and out of) the operational area. They moved bridge sections and recovered $7,315,000 worth of downed aircraft.

The withdrawal of the 1st Cavalry from Cambodia, perhaps the most critical of all its Cambodian operations, best illustrated the use of the cargo helicopters. The withdrawal sequence was time-phased to allow for the redeployment of one fire support base each day. This phasing would allow for a realistic spreading of the aircraft schedules, particularly the CH-54 Sky Cranes of the 273rd Aviation Company which were required for the movement of bridges, 155 mm howitzers, ½-ton trucks and bulldozers. On the second day of the extraction, while lifting the 1st Battalion, 50th Cavalry, from Fire Support Base David, the aviation units ran into extremely poor weather with ceilings at zero, fog and rain. The Chinooks from the 228th Assault Support Helicopter Battalion showed the ultimate in professionalism by flying at extremely low levels through the valleys, skirting the fog-covered hills, to extract the unit.

SIKORSKY H-34 SERIES

Origin Sikorsky Aircraft, Division of United Aircraft Corporation, Stratford, Connecticut **Mission** General purpose helicopter **Service** US Army (CH-34 Choctaw), US Navy (LH-34 and SH-34 Seabat), US Marine Corps (UH-34 and VH-34 Seahorse)

Engine One 1,525 hp Wright R-1820 84 B/D; **Rotor diameter** 56 ft 8 in (17.25 m); **Overall length** 46 ft 9 in (14.23 m); **Width** (blades folded) 12 ft 11 in (3.92 m); **Overall height** 15 ft 11 in (4.84 m); **Weight** (empty) 7,900 lbs (3,583 kg), (loaded) 13,000 lbs (5,897 kg) (UH-34D); **Maximum speed** (loaded, at sea level) 122 mph (196 km/h) (UH-34D); **Cruising speed** (loaded) 97 mph (156 km/h) (UH-34D); **Range** (loaded, with reserves) 247 miles (398 km) (UH-34D); **Armament** None; **Accommodation** Two crew, dual control, seated in compartment above main cabin which carried 16-18 troops, eight stretchers, or supplies.

The H-34, which was basically the Sikorsky S-58, was supplied at the time of the Vietnam War in the following versions:

CH-34A (formerly H-34A) Choctaw, the transport and general purpose helicopter in service with the US Army, armed experimentally with rockets and machine-guns.

An early version of the US Army H-34 'Choctaw' stands in front of a hangar at Fort Lewis, Washington.

CH-34C (formerly H-34C) Choctaw, similar to the CH-34A, and fitted with airborne search equipment.

LH-34D (formerly HSS-1L), a US Navy Seabat adapted for winter conditions.

UH-34D (formerly HUS-1) Seahorse, a utility version first accepted into service by the Marine Corps in January 1957, firing experimentally Bullpup missiles. Altogether 519 were completed by January 1964.

UH-34D (formerly HUS-1Z), a Seahorse fitted out for VIP travel.

UH-34E (formerly HUS-1A) Seahorse, a version of the UH-34 fitted with pontoons for emergency operation from water and during amphibious assaults.

SH-34G (formerly HSS-1) Seabat, an anti-submarine version accepted into service by the US Navy in February 1954.

SH-34J (formerly HSS-1N) Seabat, a version of the SH-34G developed for the US Navy utilizing Sikorsky automatic stabilization equipment and suitable for day and night instrument flying.

The first prototype of the H-34 flew on 8 March 1954, and the first production machine on 20 September 1954. Of the various types in service, including the US Coast Guard and commercial operators, the Marine Corps had the largest supply. With its four-blade, all-metal main and tail rotors, the H-34 was a sturdy helicopter with a semi-monocoque structure, primarily of magnesium and aluminium alloys but with some titanium and stainless steel. The pilots sat side by side operating the machine by dual control. The H-34 was supplied to ten foreign nations and gas-turbined versions were produced by Westland in the UK under the name Wessex.

As has been remarked elsewhere in this handbook, the first Marine helicopter squadron arrived in South Vietnam in April 1962 and was first stationed at Soc Trang in the Mekong Delta, although 16 US Army H-34 Choctaws were in South-east Asia as early as March 1961. These Choctaws, which were based at Udorn in Thailand, were provided for Air America, the CIA-sponsored 'company with government contracts', to fly men and material in South-east Asia. President Kennedy, who was closely watching events in Laos at the time, did not want to involve American personnel in Laos, but the Choctaws, flown by civilian crews, were available for rescue missions should the need arise.

The Marine UH-34D, or Seahorse, gained prominence in Vietnam as a search and rescue helicopter and a re-supply aircraft which on 6-7 March 1964 went to the aid of the Green Berets besieged at Nam Dong, and between 20 January and 1 April 1968 also played an important part transporting supplies in to the Marines and ARVN holding out at Khe Sanh. During the siege, UH-34s, CH-46s and UH-IEs were subjected to a murderous

Above *Marines of the 1st Battalion, 7th Marines, disembarked from UH-34 helicopters pause after an unopposed landing in a rice paddy during Operation 'Nevada' on the Batangan Peninsula in April 1966.*

Below *In the South China Sea, US Marine Corps UH-34 Seahorse helicopters line the deck of the Amphibious Assault Ship USS Iwo Jima (LPH-2) in February 1967.*

barrage by North Vietnam Army heavy automatic weapons emplaced on the tops of surrounding hills.

In the early 'advisory years', the USAF Air Rescue Service was restricted in its activities by political considerations. Since the US aircrews were supposedly conducting training missions only, there should have been little chance that anyone would be shot down. The presence of regular search and rescue forces, however, complete with helicopters and HU-16 amphibious craft, advertised the existence of air operations with a casualty potential far greater than that to be expected in the course of normal flight training. A small Search and Rescue Centre was, nevertheless, set up at Tan Son Nhut Air Base, Saigon, in December 1961.

As the pace quickened in the Vietnam conflict, the USAF was painstaking in its efforts to pick up downed flyers, and many aircraft and lives were lost in these gallant attempts, often carried out in the face of Viet Cong fire. One typical rescue operation involving Marine H-34 helicopters began on the afternoon of 8 October 1963, when two T-28 Nomads of the 4400th Combat Crew Training Squadron, code-named 'Farm Gate', rolled in on a target in the mountainous jungle area west of Danang near the Laotian jungle. One of the T-28s piloted by Americans went out of control when making a bomb run and the aircraft disintegrated on impact with the ground.

The pilot of the second aircraft returned to base and reported the loss of the T-28, which had crashed near a swollen stream that flowed into the Buong River. When the report reached Major Alan W. Saunders, Commander, Detachment 3, Pacific Air Rescue Centre, at his Saigon office, he immediately left for Danang to organize the rescue bid. On arrival, he was told that two Marine H-34s had flown to the crash site only a few hours earlier and disappeared in an area known as 'VC Valley'.

At dawn on the 9th, H-34s lifted two Vietnamese Infantry companies to the area of the downed aircraft, and as the helicopters landed enemy troops firing from the surrounding hillsides wounded three US Marine crewmen and killed a Vietnamese soldier. 'Farm Gate' T-28s, B-26s and a Vietnamese Air Force A-1 Skyraider responded by strafing the enemy positions. An American L-19 light observation plane directing the strike aircraft was hit, but managed a forced landing in friendly territory. Meanwhile, the South Vietnamese Army force began to hack out a larger landing zone to facilitate further landings.

When that task was finished, the troops began to work their way to the site of the H-34 crashes, reaching the downed choppers the next morning, 10 October, only to find the remains of ten of the twelve persons who had been aboard the two aircraft. The other two, if they had survived, had probably been carried off by the Viet

It took two days, with a battle raging nearby, for a Marine Aircraft Group (MAG)-16 maintenance crew to dismantle a troop-carrying UH-34D helicopter so that a larger CH-37 could carry it home. This action took place within ten miles of Danang in October 1965.

Cong. On 11 October, more Marine helicopters airlifted Major Saunders and his rescue team to the landing zone where they located heavy fire from hostile forces nearby. The pilots diverted to a clear area along the stream about 2½ miles north of the T-28 wreckage, from whence Major Saunders led his party through the dense jungle undergrowth, avoiding trails to lessen the risk of encountering Viet Cong booby traps. It was several hours before they hacked their way to the partially submerged wreckage of the T-28, but there was no sign of the two crewmen. After picking up the party, one of the H-34s was hit but fortunately all on board were retrieved by another H-34. The South Vietnamese Army troops in the clearing spent the night in Viet Cong territory before being lifted out the following morning.

On 15 October, Major Saunders, this time assisted by a Green Beret team and a South Vietnam Army Ranger unit, returned in H-34s to the landing zone in another effort to find any clues to the fate of the crew. Enemy resistance slowed their progress, so they did not reach the T-28 wreckage until the following day. When the party reached the crash site, the Viet Cong launched a heavy attack which was broken up by the Rangers taking up positions on a ridgeline overlooking the shattered aircraft.

After the area was finally cleared of Viet Cong, Major Saunders organized an intensive search that lasted three days, but other than the pilot's headset no sign of the missing men was ever found. Saunders believed that either the Viet Cong had killed the two men, or they had been carried away in the fast-moving waters of the swollen stream. A helicopter then extracted the search team without further loss.

SIKORSKY S-61

(S-61A, S-61B, S-61F, S-61R)

Origin Sikorsky Aircraft, Division of United Aircraft Corporation, Stratford, Connecticut **Mission** All-weather transport, search and rescue helicopter **Service** US Navy (UH-3 and SH-3D Sea King), US Air Force Air Rescue and Recovery Service (HH-3E Jolly Green Giant)

HH-3 and SH-3D SEA KING

Engine Two General Electric T58-GE-10 1,400 shp shaft-turbine; **Rotor diameter** 62 ft (18.89 m); **Overall length** 72 ft 8 in (22.14 m); **Width** (rotors folded) 16 ft 4 in (4.97 in); **Overall height** 16 ft 10 in (5.12 m); **Weight** (empty) 9,763 lbs (4,428 kg), (loaded) 21,500 lbs (9,752 kg); **Maximum speed** (loaded, at sea level) 166 mph (267 km/h); **Cruising speed** (loaded) 136 mph (219 km/h); **Range** (loaded, with reserves) 625 miles (1,005 km); **Armament** Provision made for 840 lbs (381 kg) of weapons, including homing torpedoes; **Accommodation** Four crew — pilot and co-pilot on flight deck, two sonar operators in cabin. The cabin seated 25-30 passengers, 15 stretcher cases, or 5,000 lbs (2,268 kg) of cargo.

HH-3 JOLLY GREEN GIANT

Engine Two General Electric T58-GE-5 1,500 shp shaft-turbine; **Rotor diameter** 62 ft (18.89 m); **Overall length** 73 ft (22.5 m); **Width** (rotors folded) 15 ft 10 in (4.82 m); **Overall height** 18 ft 1 in (5.51 m); **Weight** (empty) 13,255 lbs (6,012 kg), (loaded) 22,050 lbs (10,002 kg); **Maximum speed** (loaded, at sea level) 162 mph (260 km/h); **Cruising speed** (loaded) 144 mph (231 km/h); **Range** (loaded, with reserves) 465 miles (748 km); **Armament** Provision for 840 lbs (381 kg) of weapons; **Accommodation** Two crew seated side by side on the flight deck, provision in the cabin for flight engineer and attendant. Normal capacity was 25 fully-equipped troops or 15 stretcher cases, but alternative arrangements accommodated 30 troops, 15 stretcher cases or 5,000 lbs (2,268 kg) of cargo.

SH-3D Sea King Navy helicopters return to the flight deck of USS Yorktown *for refuelling and fresh crews in 1968.* Yorktown *was normally employed in the anti-submarine role.*

The Sikorsky S-61 series of twin-turbine helicopters included military and commercial variants. On 6 March 1965, an SH-3A made the first non-stop flight by helicopter across the North American continent and, in doing so, set up a new international straight-line distance record of 2,166 miles (3,485 km). The helicopter took off from the aircraft carrier *Hornet* at San Diego, California, and landed on the carrier *Franklin D. Roosevelt* at Jacksonville, Florida.

A total of more than 610 military and civilian S-61s of all types had been delivered by Sikorsky by January 1970. The only difference between the SH-3A (formerly HSS-2) and the SH-3D Sea King was that the latter had a higher rated shaft-turbine engine.

The series mission of these amphibious, all-weather aircraft was in the US Navy anti-submarine operations, but the absence of enemy submarines in Vietnam waters made the Sea King redundant in its true role. However, the US Navy recognized its use as a search and rescue helicopter, and although the Jolly Green Giant stole the limelight in picking up downed airmen, the US Navy frequently demonstrated the Sea King's search and rescue capability. Navy air units, operating from carriers in the Gulf of Tonkin, flew Sikorsky SH-3 helicopters with A-1 Skyraiders for rescue escort. Additionally, ships could be called upon to pick up survivors in the water. Although the Seventh Fleet task force commander was designated the search and rescue coordinator for the Gulf of Tonkin area north of the demilitarized zone, the Joint Search and Rescue Control Center at Tan Son Nhut exercised overall direction for search and rescue.

All these joint Air Force and Navy rescue efforts were in evidence between 5 and 8 November 1965 when Oak 01, an F-105 Thunderchief returning from a mission near Hanoi, flew into a cloud and disappeared. The 'Thud's' wingman reported Oak 01's last known position, but no anti-aircraft fire, missile firings or explosion. Because of the rapidly deteriorating weather and approaching darkness, no rescue attempt was made until dawn when, under clearing skies, Sandy 11 and Sandy 12, a pair of A-1s, flew over North Vietnam to where Oak 01 had disappeared. Anti-aircraft fire hit Sandy 12 and the pilot ejected, but Sandy 11 circled and soon spotted the pilot on the ground. Jolly Green 85, designated CH-3C and commanded by Capt Warren R. Lilly, was *en route* to the survivor as two more A-1s scrambled from the Royal Thai Air Force Base at Udorn to form a search and rescue task force. Enemy small arms fire cut into Jolly 85 as it neared the survivor, but Lilly managed to raise his badly damaged helicopter to an altitude sufficient for the crew to bail out.

As the Sandys circled, Lilly activated the automatic pilot and

A SH-3D Sea King helicopter of the US Navy from Helicopter Combat Support Squadron (HC-1) Number 1 takes off from the flight deck of the nuclear-powered attack aircraft carrier USS Enterprise (CVAN-65) in the South Pacific in January 1972.

made his way to the door. Pilots in the A-1s reported that four parachutes had opened and soon made voice and beeper contact with the downed crewmen. Normally, since rescue helicopters usually flew in pairs to meet such emergencies, the second chopper — the high bird — would have swooped in for the recovery, but because of mechanical problems no Jolly Green was available for this particular mission.

Help, however, was on its way. A US Navy Sikorsky SH-3 Sea King helicopter, Nimble 62, reported that it was flying towards the crash scene from the carrier *Independence*. Two A-1s, Sandys 13 and 14, flew to intercept the Sea King and escort it into the rescue area; they rendezvoused with Nimble 62 just east of the Vietnamese coast and flew alongside it over the beach and westwards towards the jungled mountains of North Vietnam. When the pilot of Sandy 14 spotted 37 mm tracers, he peeled off into a cloud in an evasive manoeuvre, and, like Oak 01, disappeared forever. Sandy 13 and Nimble 62 searched the area but found no sign of wreckage or survivors, and when their fuel ran low the A-1s returned to Udorn and Nimble 62 flew back to its carrier.

After refuelling, Nimble 62, with an escort of Navy A-1s, returned to search for Sandy 14, but after an hour without contact with the missing pilot they flew on to the wreckage of Jolly Green 85. At dusk, just before abandoning the search until dawn, a Navy A-1 pilot monitored a beeper's signal. As darkness engulfed the circling task force, Nimble 62 dipped down for a tree-top level visual search and the co-pilot spotted a tiny light. He ordered the penetrator down to pick up the parajumper from Jolly Green 85. The A-1s and the helicopter, with an Air Force sergeant — who would be forever grateful to the US Navy and his cigarette lighter — safely aboard, returned to *Independence*.

The early rays of the morning sun reflected off the Gulf of Tonkin as Nimble 62 and its A-1 escort took off from the carrier's deck and set a course to return to the Jolly Green 85 wreckage. As the coast of North Vietnam came into view, an orbiting US Air Force radar picket plane issued a Mig alert — enemy jets were airborne for an intercept attempt. Fishermen on sampans were clearly visible from the helicopter and its escort flew just above the waves then skimmed over the beaches to the jungle where they encountered intense small arms fire. Bullets tore into Nimble 62's fuselage and the pilot was forced to make a controlled landing inside North Vietnam.

The downed aircrew grabbed their M-16s and prepared to fight for their lives, while the A-1s blasted enemy troops moving towards the wreckage. Meanwhile, a second Sea King scrambled from *Independence* and a CH-3C left its operating base in Laos. The North Vietnamese moved an anti-aircraft gun into the area and the A-1 pilots suddenly realized they were involved in a shoot-out. Heavily damaged, the two Skyraiders limped southward to make gear-up belly landings at Danang. Meanwhile, the Sea King raced to the crash site and rescued all the survivors. Additional A-1s from the carrier then demolished the downed chopper to prevent it falling into enemy hands.

Meanwhile, encouraged by the rescue of the parajumper, the search for other survivors of Jolly Green 85 continued. Late on the afternoon of 7 November, an Air Force Sandy pilot heard a beeper signal, but darkness precluded pinpointing the source. Throughout the night, in operations rooms at Udorn and Nakhon Phanom, at the Joint Search and Rescue Center in Saigon and Rescue Control Center at Danang, as well as aboard *Independence*, intelligence officers, operations officers, and pilots planned the next day's efforts. On flight lines and in hangars throughout South Vietnam and Thailand, as well as in the bowels of *Independence*, mechanics and armourers prepared their aircraft.

In the jungles of North Vietnam, the enemy cleaned their weapons and rested before the inevitable fight. An aerial task force

A Sikorsky HH-3E medium helicopter of the US Air Force is seen with its in-flight refuelling probe in 1969.

of A-1s, CH-3Cs and SH-3s rose with the sun and converged on the Jolly Green crash site. Meanwhile, Air Force F-100s from Danang and Navy F-8 Crusaders from *Independence* flew towards their assigned anti-Mig combat patrol orbit, as the A-1s flew low over the helicopter wreckage. They finally picked up the sound of a beeper, and as the two Skyraider pilots were concentrating on the signal, enemy gunfire ripped almost simultaneously into both aircraft.

While the two damaged A-1s returned to Udorn, other Skyraiders strafed the enemy gunners who answered with 23 mm, 37 mm and small arms fire. Meanwhile, rescue controllers in Saigon and at the Rescue Control Centers at Udorn and Danang decided that further efforts would only result in additional casualties, so grudgingly they called off the rescue operations. Their decision, though a painful one, was correct. Captain Warren Lilly, Lt Jerry Singleton and SSgt Arthur Cromier, captured soon after parachuting into the jungle, were already miles away on their way to prison camps in the Hanoi area.

The Sikorsky S-61R, whose US military designation was CH-3 and HH-3 (Jolly Green Giants), although based on the SH-3A introduced many important design changes. These included provision of a hydraulically operated rear ramp for straight loading of wheeled vehicles, a 2,000 lb (907 kg) capacity winch for internal cargo handling, retractable tricycle-type landing gear, pressurized rotor blades for quick and easy inspection, gas-turbine auxiliary

A US Air Force Air Rescue and Recovery Service Sikorsky HH-3E 'Jolly Green Giant' helicopter at Eglin Air Force Base, Florida, in 1967.

power supply for independent field operations, self-lubricating main and tail rotors and built-in equipment for the removal and replacement of all major components in remote areas.

The CH-3E designation became applicable in February 1966 following the introduction of the uprated engines (1,500 shp T58-GE-5s). A new pod-mounted turret armament system was also developed for this version, with the weapon located off each sponson and gunsights at the port and starboard personnel doors. Each pod mounted an Emerson Electric TAT-102 turret, incorporating a General Electric six-barrel T 62 mm minigun and an 8,000-round ammunition storage-feed system. More than 180 degrees traverse was achieved on each side of the aircraft to give complete 360 degree coverage with overlapping fire forward.

The HH-3E, allocated to the USAF Air Rescue and Recovery Service, was fitted with additional equipment comprising armour, self-sealing fuel tanks, a retractable flight refuelling probe, defensive armament (two mini-machine-guns) and rescue hoist. The armour plating and self-sealing fuel tanks helped to protect the crew if a hovering helicopter was hit by ground fire. In terms of speed and ceiling the HH-3E resembled the CH-3E, but the former carried auxiliary fuel tanks which extended its range to 625 miles (1,005 km). Mid-air refuelling was also introduced because the Jolly Green Giant at first still lacked the capacity to loiter long over the search and rescue area.

Adopted in 1967, the HC-130P (Hercules)/HH-3E demonstrated an eight-hour mission and then began flying daily operations. Its externally fitted variable-speed hoist with a 240 ft (73.15 m) long cable was stressed to lift 600 lb (272.16 kg). Operating out of Udorn or Danang, the Jolly Green Giant could fly to any point in North Vietnam and return home in one flight.

SIKORSKY S-65A

Origin Sikorsky Aircraft, Division of United Aircraft Corporation, Stratford, Connecticut **Mission** Twin-turbine heavy assault transport helicopter, search and rescue. **Service** US Navy (CH-53A Sea Stallion), USAF Air Rescue and Recovery Service (HH-53B/C Super Jolly Green Giant), US Marine Corps (CH-53D)

Engine Normally powered by two General Electric 64-GE-6 shaft-turbines mounted on pods on each side of the main rotor pylon. The CH-53A could utilize without air frame modification the T64-GE-1 3,080 shp or the T64-GE-16 (mod) 3,435 shp engines; **Rotor diameter** 72 ft 3 in (22.02 m); **Overall length** (rotors turning) 88 ft 3 in (26.89 m); **Overall width** (rotors folded) 15 ft 6 in (4.72 m); **Overall height** 24 ft 11 in (7.58 m); **Weight** (empty) 22,444 lbs (10,180 kg) (CH-53A), 23,485 lbs (10,652 kg) (CH-53D), 23,125 lbs (10,489 kg) (HH-53B), 23,257 lbs (10,549 kg) (HH-53C), (loaded) 35,000 lbs (15,876 kg) (CH-53A), 36,400 lbs (16,511 kg) (CH-53D), 37,400 lbs (16,964 kg) (HH-53B), 37,446 lbs (16,985 kg) (HH-35C); **Maximum speed** (loaded, at sea level) 198 mph (318 km/h) (CH-53A), 196 mph (315 km/h) (CH-53D), 186 mph (299 km/h) (HH-53B, HH-53C); **Cruising speed** (loaded) 175 mph (281 km/h), (CH-53A), 173 mph (278 km/h) (CH-53D, HH-53B, HH-53C); **Range** (loaded, with reserves) 257 miles (413 km) (CH-53A, CH-53D), 540 miles (869 km) (HH-53B, HH-53C); **Armament** Three 7.62 mm miniguns (HH-53B, HH-53C); **Accommodation** Three crew, 38 combat-equipped troops in main cabin in forward-facing seats with additional provision for 24 stretchers and four medical orderlies.

A Marine CH-53 Sea Stallion helicopter places a 105-mm howitzer of the 12th Marine Regiment atop a mountain fire base position southwest of An Hoa. The 12th Marines were supporting Operation 'Taylor Common' in 1968.

A Sikorsky CH-53 Sea Stallion of Marine Heavy Helicopter Squadron 463, operating from Quang Tri, prepares to lift a damaged CH-46 Sea Knight after the helicopter was downed by enemy fire in 1968. The Sea Knight had been involved in operations in support of ground units in the northern tier of I Corps.

On 27 August 1962, it was announced that Sikorsky had been selected by the US Navy to produce a heavy assault transport helicopter for use by the US Marine Corps. The first flight was made on 14 October 1964, and deliveries began in mid-1966. Designated CH-53A, this aircraft used many of the components of the Sikorsky CH-54 Tarhe (Sky Crane) (see page 113) but it was powered by two T64 shaft-turbine engines and had a watertight hull. A full-size rear opening with built-in ramp, permitted easy loading and unloading, with the aid of a special internal roller-skid hydraulically-operated, heavy cargo track combination.

The CH-53A, which commenced service in Vietnam in January 1967, was intended to operate in all weather and climatic conditions, to take account of the abrupt seasonal changes in South-east Asia. It was initially envisaged that the CH-53A would carry two Hawk missiles complete with cable reels and control console, but its usual loads in Vietnam included two jeeps or a 105 mm gun and carriage. An external cargo system permitted in-flight pick-up and release without ground assistance. The Sea Stallion's main rotor blades and tail pylon folded hydraulically for stowage on board ship.

The CH-53A introduced several innovations and achieved various helicopter records. On 17 February 1968, a CH-53A with General Electric T64-16 (modified) engines flew carrying 28,500 lbs (12,927 kg) of payload and fuel (a gross weight of 51,900 lbs (23,541 kg)), establishing new unofficial payload and gross weight records for a production helicopter built outside the Soviet Union. On 26 April 1968, a Marine Corps CH-53A made the first automatic terrain clearance flight in helicopter history and subsequently concluded flight tests of an Integrated Helicopter Avionics System (IHAS). On 23 October 1968, a Marine Corps CH-53A performed a series of loops and rolls as part of a joint Naval Air Systems Command and Sikorsky flight test programme aimed at investigating the CH-53A's rotor systems dynamics and manoeuvrability characteristics.

In September 1966, the USAF ordered eight HH-53B heavy lift helicopters for its Aerospace Rescue and Recovery Service. The first of these flew on 15 March 1967 and deliveries began in June 1967. The HH-53B, which, like the HH-53C, gained the nickname Super Jolly Green Giant, was powered by two 3,080 shp T64-GE-3 shaft-turbine engines. It had the same general equipment as the HH-3E (Jolly Green Giant), including a retractable flight refuelling probe, jettisonable auxiliary fuel tanks and armament.

On 3 August 1968, Sikorsky delivered the first HH-53C helicopter to the USAF. This was an improved version of the HH-53B with 3,435 shp T64-GE-7 engines, auxiliary jettisonable fuel tanks, each of 450 US gallons (1,703 litres) capacity on new cantilever mounts, a flight refuelling probe and a rescue hoist with 250 ft (76.2 m) of cable. An external cargo hook of 20,000 lbs (9,072 kg) capacity allowed the HH-53C to recover Apollo spacecraft. The self-sealing bladder fuel tanks housed in the forward part of the sponsons of the S-65A series gave added protection to the crews if hit by small arms fire from the ground.

The CH-53D, assigned for service with the US Marine Corps, was first delivered on 3 March 1969, and was an improved version of the CH-53A with two T64-GE-412 or T64-GE-413 engines. The former had a military rating of 3,695 shp and the latter a maximum rating of 3,925 shp. A total of 64 troops could if necessary be accommodated in a high-density arrangement, while an integral cargo handling system made it possible for one man to load or unload one short ton of palletized cargo per minute. The main rotor and tail pylon folded automatically for carrier operations.

A CH-53 Sea Stallion helicopter of the Marine Corps lifts an OV-10A Bronco Short Take-Off and Landing (VSTOL) two-seat observation and COIN (COunter-INsurgency) aircraft during exercises near the Patuxent River, Maryland, USA, in 1969. The North American OV-10 Bronco proved an effective weapon against the Viet Cong.

An excellent example of the deployment of the 'Giants' in assault and rescue roles was provided on the night of 20 November 1970 when a mini-armada of aircraft took off from Udorn, Thailand, heading for a location 28 miles (45 km) north-west of Hanoi. One hour before midnight, pilots, navigators, pararescuemen, radio operators, flight mechanics and engineers, together with a small group of assault troops, boarded two C-130 Hercules transports, an HH-3 Jolly Green Giant and five HH-53 Super Jolly Green Giant helicopters.

This contingent, which was airborne in ten minutes, became the centre of a task force that included five A-1E Skyraiders, five F-105 Thunderchiefs and ten F-4 Phantoms heading north-eastwards towards the enemy heartland. Meanwhile, from the Gulf of Tonkin a diversionary force of Navy F-4 Phantoms, A-4 Skyhawks and A-6 Intruders flew towards Haiphong and the eastern coastal cities.

The purpose of this mission was to rescue up to a hundred prisoners of war from the suffering and despair they had experienced at Son Tay prison. It was an operation unique in concept and bold in planning.

Plans for the Son Tay raid had begun on 5 June 1970. To achieve surprise, it was decided to crash-land a helicopter loaded with shock troops directly into a small compound within the camp confines. Because of the trees in the compound, this helicopter would be damaged and would have to be left behind, so an older chopper like the UH-1 was considered. However, this idea was discarded because of the Huey's limitation in range and accommodation capacity in favour of the HH-3E Jolly Green Giant, which could carry enough troops to keep the guards busy while other Rangers blasted a hole in the prison's outside wall so that the assault forces landing around the compound could get in to search the cells. Due to be phased out of service the following month, the HH-3 would certainly go out in a blaze of glory!

Training for the flight part of the mission began on 20 August at Eglin Air Force Base, Florida, where the crews concentrated on night formation flying. By early September, 92 assault troops joined with the Air Force to begin their part of the training, which included attacks on a mock-up structure made of wood and cloth which was erected every night and taken down before dawn to keep Soviet photo reconnaissance satellites from spotting it.

Aircrews for the C-130Es and A-1Es worked out their portions of the mission; the former were to provide navigational assistance to and from the camp. Also, when these aircraft reached Son Tay the plan called for a pallet loaded with napalm canisters to form a flaming pool and act as a reference point for other aircraft. The A-1Es would also carry specially configured napalm canisters which, upon bursting, would also form flaming pools, just in case the C-130s did not have a chance to drop their pallet. Also, the A-1Es were to bomb a bridge near the camp to slow down any enemy force that might try to intervene.

On 10 November, the task force began to move from Eglin to Takhli Royal Thai Air Force Base, seven HH-53s and two HH-3Es being assigned as primary and back-up helicopters. Weather stepped in to determine the final hour of the raid — Typhoon Patsy had been building up over the South China Sea and was bearing down on North Vietnam. By 21 November, the original target date, the Gulf of Tonkin would be too rough for aircraft carrier operations, and the Navy would not be able to make diversionary flights to confuse the North Vietnamese. Late on the morning of 20 November, the task force was ordered to mount the raid one day early — that night.

When the two C-130s, the HH-3E and the five HH-53s were

airborne at about 2310 hours Udorn time, they set course for North Vietnam. At the first ridge of mountains north of Vientane, they flew into clouds, and the choppers spread out to give each other room. The single Jolly, flown by Col Herbert R. Zehnder and Maj Herbert D. Kalen, stayed behind the leading C-130, riding the crest of its propwash like a racing car in the slipstream of a preceding vehicle, otherwise it would have been too slow to keep pace with the C-130s and HH-53s.

As the choppers crossed northern Laos and approached North Vietnamese radar coverage, a vast force of 116 mission support aircraft took off from seven bases in Thailand and three carriers in the Gulf of Tonkin. Five F-105 Wild Weasels passed the task force to reach the Son Tay area early in order to keep the surface-to-air (SAM) missile sites from acquiring fixes or radar locks on the approaching aircraft, while ten F-4Ds from Udorn remained in Mig combat orbit over north-eastern Laos. Eight KC-135 tankers orbited near the F-4s ready to fuel the jets, and two others were standing by over the Gulf of Tonkin to provide the same service for the Navy jets. Two Lockheed EC-121Ds, four-engine Constellation transports used by the Air Force as Early Warning/Ground Control Intercept and Mig warning aircraft, flew along the Laos/North Vietnam border gathering intelligence on enemy fighter reactions. Finally, three RE-135 Combat Apple Electronic Intelligence Collection aircraft from the Strategic Air Command provided communications support which included relaying messages to the National Military Command Center in the Pentagon.

The raiders entered the objective area at less than 500 ft (152 m), and the C-130s led the six choppers until nightbound Son Tay lay only a few miles ahead. At that point, the leading C-130 climbed to 1,500 ft (457 m) followed by two Super Jolly Green Giants: Apple 4, piloted by Lt Col Royal H. Brown and Maj Ryland R. Dreibelbis, and Apple 5 with Maj Kenneth D. Murphy and Capt William M. McGeorge at the controls. Brown's Apple 4 was the primary flare chopper and one of those designated to haul back the released prisoners, while Apple 5 was the secondary flare helicopter.

Over the Son Tay compound the flares worked perfectly, so the two choppers flew to a planned orbit area nearby while the C-130 circled to drop a fire-fight simulator (firecrackers with tin fuses) on an army engineer school near the prison. It then released its pallet of napalm before flying off to its designated orbit. The second C-130, only a minute behind the first, went in leading the five A-1s. After the A-1s pulled away, the C-130 dropped a napalm marker and then joined the other C-130 in its orbit, while Skyraiders bombed the nearby bridge before taking up their orbit over the flaming pool of napalm.

A Navy CH-53A Sea Stallion of Helicopter Mine Countermeasure Squadron 12 (HM-12) in 1973, one of many Sea Stallions employed during Operation 'End Sweep'. The objective was to clear mines from North Vietnamese harbours and in-land waterways, as stipulated by the Paris Peace Treaty signed in January of that year.

In most operations something goes wrong, and the Son Tay raid was to be no different in that respect. In the third helicopter, Apple 3, flown by Maj Frederick M. Donahue and Capt Thomas R. Waldron, an instrument panel light labelled 'transmission' flicked on. Both men knew that the transmission is the most vital piece of machinery in any helicopter, that it could disintegrate in a matter of seconds, and if that happened the chopper would crash. Instrument panel lights, however, often short, causing them to flicker on when nothing, in fact, is happening.

Donahue weighed the factors. Normally he would declare an emergency and land the chopper in the first available safe spot until he could determine if anything was indeed amiss in the transmission. These, however, were not normal circumstances, and if he declared an emergency and pulled out of the operation the entire mission might be jeopardized. Consequently, he coolly told his co-pilot 'Ignore the sonofabitch'.

In those few seconds of confusion, Donahue had let Apple 3 drift slightly off course. The helicopter was now directly on course for the sapper school instead of the Son Tay prison, some 400 yards beyond. Donahue realized his mistake and wheeled his chopper north to the camp. In Banana 1, the HH-3E just behind Apple 3, Col Zehnder and Maj Kalen did not realize that they were over the wrong compound until they had settled down inside its walls and the gunner had blasted the gun towers. When the pilots realized their mistake, they poured on the power, lifted their chopper over the school's walls and headed for the camp.

In Apple 1, Lt Col Warner A. Britton and Maj Alfred C. Montrem were too busy concentrating on landing and getting a stuck rear ramp down to hear the radio warnings from Donahue and Zehnder. After a few minutes, Col Arthur 'Bull' Simons, who was leading this assault group and who was in overall command of the troops, realized he and his men were in the wrong compound, but by this time his troops had breached the wall and were inside the courtyard encountering very heavy opposition. Nevertheless, 'Bull' Simons gathered his men and beat a hasty retreat back to the landing zone.

Meanwhile, Britton and Montrem had relaxed enough to hear the frantic calls of their comrades warning them they had assaulted the wrong target. Britton spun the chopper round and rushed back to the landing zone just as Simons and his troops arrived. Within three minutes they were loaded up and off to the Son Tay compound. 'Bull' Simon's section claimed after the raid that they had killed scores of NVA troops and Russian and Chinese advisers, but as the enemy encountered were clad in their black pyjamas no one could be certain who the incumbents of the army engineer school really were.

Back at the Son Tay prison compound, the battle raged. First, Donahue flew Apple 3 across the prison blasting the guard towers with its miniguns. Zehnder brought Banana 1 in quickly on Apple 3's heels; Herb Kalen, the co-pilot, cut the engines at precisely the right second and the HH-3E dropped into the compound, swinging around on its rotors as the blades sliced into a huge tree, just as expected. When it hit the ground, troops rushed out down the rear ramp, each running to his assigned objective. Above the roar of battle, a bullhorn sounded and an officer kept shouting 'Keep down! We're Americans'.

Inside the cell houses, two-man teams began to systematically clear each cell block. One team broke in on the camp commandant and shot him in his bed where he lay, and all the North Vietnamese caught were killed. Nine minutes after the landing the first assault team reported 'negative items' — no POWs. Three minutes later all teams had reported the same 'negative items'. The stark truth was that there were no American POWs in the Son Tay prison camp. It was later learned that the prisoners had been transferred to another camp when the monsoon rains had somehow affected the water supply on which the camp depended, and this humanitarian gesture had thus led to the failure of the American Son Tay rescue effort.

A Sea Stallion tows a Mark 105 magnetic hydrofoil minesweeping device during a training flight before the commencement of Operation 'End Sweep' in March 1973. Helicopters and ocean minesweepers combined for the operation which took six months to complete.

'End Sweep': a Sea Stallion tows a minesweeping magnetic orange pipe (MK-1B) from the hold of the Amphibious Transport Dock, USS Dubuque (LPO-2).

People in Son Tay village heard the fire-fight simulators and the aircraft overhead, and watched as 16 SAMs arched across the sky. For half an hour they saw the napalm burning and the aircraft circling above. One man home on leave from the army, when subsequently captured in South Vietnam, told US Air Force interrogators that he saw tanks moving toward the camp just as the last chopper pulled away. Above and to the west, victims of those 16 SAMs, two F-105s were damaged. One of them limped back to Udorn to make an emergency landing, and the other flew towards Udorn but, over northern Laos, the crew ejected.

In the darkness over western North Vietnam, a Mig was seeking the remnants of the task force heading back toward Thailand when his air intercept radar found Apple 4 piloted by Lt Col Royal H. Brown. When Brown realized that his chopper was under attack, he put it into a violent turning dive. The Mig pilot fired a heat-seeking missile, but it streaked past the twisting helicopter to hit a hill. With the HH-53 turning and manoeuvring close to the ground, the hunter soon realized he would not be able to find his prey and turned for home.

It was almost 0300 hours when Apple 4 found Apple 5, flown by Maj Kenneth D. Murphy, and together they continued toward Udorn. Suddenly they received a Mayday call from the F-105 in trouble over Laos. These two choppers, slated to carry back the prisoners, were empty, so they rendezvoused with Lime 01, an HC-130P tanker, refuelled and flew toward the downed crewmen. An Air America C-123 Provider also arrived and began to drop flares. Although the rescue choppers searched, they could not spot the survivors.

When they started to pick up small arms fire, the HC-130P, acting as airborne mission control, ordered them to orbit with him until dawn. About three hours passed before the sunrise brought four A-1s from Nakhon Phanom. The leading Sandy soon located both men, ordered his three wingmen to strafe the area and then told the choppers to make their pick-ups. Apple 4 got the 'Thud's' GIB ('guy in back') and Apple 5 picked up the pilot, then both choppers refuelled and headed for Udorn.

Success cannot always be measured by unqualified triumphs. The Son Tay raid was a tactical success in that the plan worked; had there been prisoners at the compound, and had the raiders met with a similar level of enemy resistance, they probably would have been rescued. Additionally, the raid showed the Hanoi leadership that their country was still quite vulnerable to attack. It also focused the attention of the world on the plight of American prisoners of war in North Vietnam. Finally, not least from the US Air Force viewpoint, the 'Giants' had done their job and performed magnificently.

VERTOL H-21 SHAWNEE

Origin Vertol Aircraft Corporation, Morton, Pennsylvania **Mission** Transportation of cargo, equipment and personnel **Service** USAF, US Army

Engine One 1,425 hp Wright R-1820-103 (H-21B, H-21C); **Rotor diameter** 44 ft (13.39 m); **Overall length** (rotors turning) 86 ft 4 in (26.27 m); **Width** (blades folded) 14 ft 4 in (4.36 m); **Overall height** 15 ft 5 in (4.69 m); **Weight** (empty) 8,900 lbs (4,037 kg), (loaded) 15,000 lbs (6,804 kg); **Maximum speed** (loaded, at sea level) 127 mph (204 km/h); **Cruising speed** (loaded) 101 mph (162.5 km/h); **Range** (loaded, with reserves) 280 miles (450 km); **Armament** Improvised; **Accommodation** Two crew and co-pilot (or medical orderly) in forward compartment, 20 troops or 12 stretchers in the cabin.

The Vertol Workhorse (the name given to the first 214 H-21s, but subsequently designated by both the USAF and US Army the H-21 Shawnee) first flew in the mid 1950s. The YH-21 and H-21A were assigned as Arctic rescue helicopters with a carrying capacity of 12 stretchers or 14 troops, while the H-21B and H-21C performed assault airlift, transportation of troops and equipment, and rescue and evacuation missions for the Air Force and Army. The Shawnee was a tandem rotor helicopter with two three-blade rotors, one above the flight deck and the other at the tip of the up-swept tail.

Under a US Navy Army contract, an H-21C aircraft was converted by fitting two General Electric T58 gas turbine engines in place of a single R-1820 piston engine. Both turbines were mounted aft in such a way that the failure of one would not affect the operation of the other. The greater power and lighter weight of this model, designated H-21D, which first flew in 1957, allowed the new helicopter a 40 per cent greater payload than the piston-engined versions of the H-21, together with a cruising speed of up to 150 mph (241 km/h) and a much higher hovering ceiling.

The first H-21s were produced by Piasecki in 1949 but production was taken over by Vertol (Vertical Take-off and Landing) Aircraft Corporation in 1955; the Workhorse finally acquired the title Boeing Vertol H-21 Shawnee. An Army Shawnee made the first non-stop helicopter flight across the United States on 24 August 1956, when a H-21C flew 2,610 miles (4,199 km) in 37 hours. Altogether, the H-21 was a production success with 557 units being constructed for the US military while 150 were constructed for foreign users.

The H-21s which were unloaded in their protective plastic material on Saigon harbour on 11 December 1961 from USS *Card*

Vietnamese and American personnel push an H-21 helicopter, which has been damaged by Viet Cong machine-gun fire, back to its hangar in South Vietnam, 1963.

were the first American helicopters to arrive in the Vietnam war zone. Termed 'additional military equipment' on the cargo manifest, the H-21 Shawnee was a growth variant of the US Navy's HRP-1 Rescuer. The Rescuer had been an ungainly tandem rotor machine with fabric covering, but the new H-21 had a fairly sleek all-metal fuselage and a number of other improvements.

The crew for the H-21 assault helicopters were seated in the nose under a large wrap-around plexiglass unit, while the space aft of the pilots was devoted to the carrying of cargo and passengers. The H-21 was one of the first helicopters with which the Army seriously began to experiment with different armament fittings. H-21s were tested with a variety of rocket pods and machine-gun combinations, one even having a remote-controlled turret added under the fuselage. In January 1962, the Shawnees gave the first demonstration of American air power when ten of them ferried a group of ARVN paratroopers and US advisers from Tan Son Nhut Air Base to attack an enemy radio base near the village of Ap Bac

A 'Flying Banana' flies South Vietnamese troops on a mission over a river south of Saigon, while an armed Huey flies in close support.

on the Plain of Reeds. The Vietnamese soldiers, who were of small stature in comparison with the average American, had to be hoisted on board by crew members.

As suspected, the Viet Cong were more than surprised by this sudden incursion of H-21s accompanied by the noise from their engines and rotors. After putting up only minimal resistance, the enemy melted away into the surrounding area, leaving the majority of their weapons, supplies and a radio transmitter that had been used to bombard Saigon with anti-government propaganda. Post-mission debriefing between the Americans and South Vietnamese saw the allies agreeing on the fact that the mission was a success, but agreeing also that the airmobile concept had some way to go to achieve perfection.

The Viet Cong were swift to appreciate the advantages of the troop helicopters, and equally quick to exploit the disadvantages. The weaknesses of the concept in those early days were that only small forces could be air-landed and, if attacked in force by the Viet Cong, would find it difficult to withdraw. Strike elements were usually unfamiliar with the terrain in their target areas, and in forested and jungle-covered mountain regions the true nature of the ground could not be discerned from the air. Low-flying choppers were vulnerable to small arms fire, and the population

An H-21 of the US Air Force fitted with floats for the sea rescue role.

was generally sympathetic to the Viet Cong.

The first Shawnees had arrived in Vietnam with glossy olive drab paint finishes and large national insignias. 'United States' was painted brightly on the fuselage and, while making a very attractive appearance overall, also made a readily observable target for the enemy — the VC had a habit of using the national insignia and 'Army' on the forward fuselage as aiming points! These bright, parade-dress markings soon began to disappear, although there was no concerted direction to put the H-21s into low visibility markings; each set of markings became the choice of the individual pilot or crew chief. Usually, whatever cans of flat dark-coloured paint were found lying around the base were appropriated and the bright markings and insignia slopped out with a paint brush.

Some of the more artistic of the helicopter crews went to considerable trouble to paint their entire helicopter in multi-coloured drab camouflage, hoping the machines would blend with the surrounding vegetation. Within a few months it was possible to view an entire H-21 unit and not find two similarly painted helicopters. Usually the national insignia was applied to the top of the fuselage where it could not be seen by enemy gunners, while some form of white stripe was also usually applied to the top of the fuselage spine to aid other pilots in spotting the choppers from above.

By the autumn of 1962, five Shawnee companies were based in South Vietnam — the 57th, 8th, 93rd, 33rd and 81st Transportation Companies (Helicopter Light). The H-21s were, however, breaking down with depressing regularity, and pilots had noted early on that the helicopter, especially when fully loaded, was underpowered. A serious shortage of spare parts was eased when a company of fixed-wing de Havilland (Canada) U-1A Otters were used to ferry spares to the Shawnee units.

As losses among the rather ponderous H-21s began to mount, the advisers began to arm their machines. Although not as elaborate as the armed H-21 testing carried out in the States, many of the Shawnees were field modified to take a mount in the main door on the left side which could hold a .30 calibre air-cooled Browning machine-gun. Sometimes a similar weapon was added to the smaller door on the forward right fuselage. Both weapons had a fairly limited range of fire and, since the door openings were already small, the ease with which troops could enter and exit was also restricted, especially when under fire. The weapons did, however, add a little moral support for the crew and, in fact, could keep the VCs' heads down when the bursts were well-directed.

In late 1962, the Army divided its five H-21 units into service in the four military regions which composed the strategic map of South Vietnam. It was in the mountain areas in the northern I Corps Tactical Zone that the Shawnee's performance suffered most, loads having to be greatly restricted to allow the big machine to lurch into the air. To help deal with this problem, a swap was instigated with the Marine Corps which saw Sikorsky H-34s (smaller but in many ways more powerful and more capable than the H-21) of HMM-362 Squadron, based at Soc Trang in the Mekong Delta, transferred to the mountain beat and the H-21s operated in the lowland areas that were more suited to their performance.

The ungainly CH-21C Shawnee, thus designated in 1962, which was likened to a 'flying banana', was, in spite of its shortcomings, the pioneer troop carrier in the US Army and made the first effective use of aerial combat weapons in Vietnam. Although slow, the CH-21Cs were relatively dependable. With the Shawnee, US Army air and ground crews had their first experience of the dirt, heat and humidity of South-east Asia, which also did nothing to help the helicopter's performance. The CH-21C was succeeded by more powerful helicopters in Vietnam, principally the tandem rotor Boeing Vertol CH-47 Chinook, and none remained in the Army inventory as the Vietnam War post-1965 got into its stride.

GLOSSARY

A
AH   Attack helicopter
Air Cav   Air Cavalry –
helicopter-borne assault
troops
AK-47   Chinese-made
automatic rifle
ARVN   Army of the
Republic of South Vietnam

B
B-40   Chinese-made
rocket
BIS   Board of Inspection
and Survey

C
C-rations   US Army combat
ration packs
Cav of the Cav   The elite
1st Squadron, 9th US
Cavalry
CH   Combat helicopter
CIDG   Civilian Irregular
Defence Group

D
DMZ   Demilitarized Zone
Dust-off   Radio code-name
for medical evacuation
helicopter

E
Eagle Flight   Air assault
team constantly on the alert
EH   Electronics helicopter
En route (phase)   Helicopter
flight to target area

G
Go-Go-Bird   Heavily armed
version of CH-47 Chinook
helicopter
Guns   Gunship

H
H   Helicopter
HAL   Navy's Helicopter
Attack (Light) Squadron
HH   Heavy helicopter
HM   Marine Heavy Lift
Helicopter Squadron
Huey   Common name for

UH-1 Bell Iroquois
helicopter

I
In-country   Slang
expression for period of tour
in Vietnam

J
JCPS   Jungle Canopy
Platform System – platform
made of steel matting
unsuccessfully used to land
helicopters on tree tops in
Vietnam jungle
JGS   Joint General Staff

L
LAMPS   Light Airborne
Mobile Surface System
LSD   Dock-landing ship
LST   Landing ship, tank
LZ   Landing Zone

M
M-16   Standard American
automatic rifle
MASH   Mobile Army
Surgical Hospital
Medevac   Medical
evacuation – removal by
helicopter of wounded from
combat zone

N
NOROC   Armoured panels
made by Norton Company
for crew protection in
helicopters
NVA   North Vietnam Army –
Communist regulars

O
OH   Observation helicopter

P
PACAF   Pacific Air
Command
PACV   Patrol air cushion
vehicle
Pink Team   AH-1
HueyCobra and other
helicopters used for special
protective screening of Air

Cavalry troops when
airborne

R
RPG 2,7   Soviet anti-tank
rockets
RSSZ   Rung Sat Special
Zone – an extensive
mangrove swamp near
Saigon used by the Viet
Cong for base areas.

S
SAC   Strategic Air
Command
SAM   Surface-to-air missile
SEAL   Navy's Sea-Air-
Land commando team
Seawolves   Navy's
helicopter squadron (HAL 3)
assigned to riverine
operations
Slick   Helicopter troop
carrier
Snake   Hueycobra AH-1
helicopter
STAB   Seal team assault
boat
STOL   Short Take-Off and
Landing

U
USMC   United States
Marine Corps
UTTCO   Utility Tactical
Transport Helicopter
Company

V
VERTREP   Vertical
replenishment (supply by
helicopter)
Viet Cong   Communist
guerrillas
Viet Minh   Forerunners of
the NVA – raised during
Second World War to fight
Japanese, and fought
against the French in the
Indochina War 1946-54
VIP   Very important person
VMO   Marine Observation
Squadron

INDEX